The Conservation of Archaeological Sites in the Mediterranean Region

An International Conference Organized by
the Getty Conservation Institute and
the J. Paul Getty Museum,
6–12 May 1995

Edited by Marta de la Torre

THE GETTY CONSERVATION INSTITUTE

LOS ANGELES

Cover: Francesco Bartolozzi, *View of the Town of Spalatro from the South West*. Etching, ca. 1760. From Robert Adam, *Ruins of the Emperor Diocletian at Spalatro in Dalmatia* (London, 1764), pl. 4. Resource Collections, Getty Research Institute for the History of Art and the Humanities, Los Angeles.

Tevvy Ball, *Managing Editor*
Sylvia Tidwell, *Copy Editor*
Deborah Lott and Robert Ruckman, *Permissions Editors*
Anita Keys, *Production Coordinator*
Jeffrey Cohen, *Series Designer*
Hespenheide Design, *Book Designer*

Printed in the United States of America
10 9 8 7 6 5 4 3 2 1

The Getty Conservation Institute, an operating program of the J. Paul Getty Trust, works internationally to further the appreciation and preservation of the world's cultural heritage for the enrichment and use of present and future generations.

Library of Congress Cataloging-in-Publication Data

The conservation of archaeological sites in the Mediterranean region : an international conference
    organized by the Getty Conservation Institute and the J. Paul Getty Museum, 6–12 May 1995 /
    edited by Marta de la Torre.
        p.   cm.
    Includes bibliographical references.
    ISBN 0-89236-486-6
      1. Historic sites—Mediterranean Region—Conservation and restoration—Congresses.
    2. Historic buildings—Mediterranean Region—Conservation and restoration—Congresses.
    3. Mediterranean Region—Antiquities—Collection and preservation—Congresses. 4. Cultural
    property, Protection of—Mediterranean Region—Congresses.   I. De la Torre, Marta, 1946– .
    II. Getty Conservation Institute.   III. J. Paul Getty Museum.
DE59.5C66   1997   97-19117
909'.09822—dc21   CIP

Contents

Preface

IN MAY 1995 the Getty Conservation Institute (GCI) and the J. Paul Getty Museum hosted a meeting of senior government officials and other specialists in the areas of culture, archaeology, and tourism from seventeen nations around the Mediterranean Sea. The purpose of the meeting was to promote the protection of the archaeological heritage through coordinated management of its appropriate uses—research, education, and tourism.

For several years, the GCI has taken a leading role in advocating the conservation of sites through balanced management of the interests and requirements of the various concerned parties. Archaeological sites are of value to individuals and groups (archaeologists, local populations, visitors, national authorities, and others) for various reasons, and decision makers can protect these values once they are recognized. In its courses and field projects, the GCI has developed a methodology for developing site management; it consists of a systematic planning process that takes into consideration many factors relating to the status of the site, the resources available, the local and national laws, and the values perceived by the various interested groups.

The J. Paul Getty Museum is committed to scholarly research on Greek and Roman antiquity and to the conservation of this heritage. The Museum and the GCI—two programs of the J. Paul Getty Trust—have complementary interests in archaeological sites, and together they endorsed the message of the conference: The archaeological heritage is valuable to professionals in archaeology and ancient history, and equally valuable, for many reasons, to citizens, tourists, government officials, and others. To conserve it and protect it from damage, those responsible for its care must understand all the reasons that make a site valuable.

The conference was designed to promote a broad, international, and interdisciplinary exchange of information, ideas, and viewpoints about protection and management of archaeological sites. The organizers hoped to explore the issues involved in the management, conservation, and presentation of sites and to encourage cooperation among the various groups. To ensure a productive exchange, invitations were extended to individuals with commitment, experience, and policy-making authority from government ministries and related agency posts, and to representatives of foreign schools of archaeology and other international organizations. The eighty individuals who attended the conference represented the various groups interested in archaeological sites. For many, it was their first opportunity to discuss their concerns with others from different disciplines, industries, and countries. The conference, which took place from 6 to 12 May 1995, was held aboard a ship; this venue helped to focus attention on the discussions at hand, to create opportunities to see several sites, and to encourage informal conversations and personal interaction among the participants. The entire assembly listened to presentations, discussed the issues in small groups, visited three heritage sites, and, at the end of the conference, formulated the Conclusions presented herein.

Progress of the Conference

The conference was formally opened on 7 May at the Carthage Museum by a representative of the minister of culture of Tunisia; John Walsh, director of the J. Paul Getty Museum; and Miguel Angel Corzo, director of the Getty Conservation Institute. The opening ceremony was followed by a panel of individuals from the region who addressed the value of archaeological sites from their distinct perspectives as representatives of governmental authorities, tourism agencies, national archaeological agencies, foreign archaeological missions, and the conservation profession. The panel discussions clearly affirmed that every site is valued from a number of perspectives—historic, scientific, social (including political and religious), economic, and aesthetic.

As the participants traveled by ship from Tunisia to Italy, Turkey, and Greece during the days that followed, four speakers addressed in depth the topics of site management, and the presentation and reconstruction of sites. The edited texts of these presentations are included herein.

An important part of the conference was the opportunity to visit three sites—Piazza Armerina, on the Italian island of Sicily; Knossos, on the Greek island of Crete; and Ephesus, in Turkey—to examine them within the context of the discussions. These sites were selected because they are affected by the conflicting requirements of scholarship, conservation, presentation, and tourism.

With these three places as examples, the participants could observe what was protected at the sites and examine the results of some management decisions. They could also see the impact of interventions, research, and presentation on the material remains and the values of the sites. Prior to each visit, the sites were introduced to conference participants by members of the Getty staff; each presentation covered the history of excavation and intervention, issues specific to the site, and current statistics on visitation and supervision. These lectures are included in this volume as well.

After each visit, the participants broke up into small groups to discuss their impressions and observations. The intimate size of the groups and the ample time allowed for discussion encouraged a free exchange of views and an in-depth exploration of issues of common concern. The discussions elucidated the particular challenges currently faced in the region, focused attention on shared concerns, and explored possible policy solutions. It became clear that even though the participants represented different nations, political opinions, legal systems, and professional backgrounds, they discovered considerable common ground in their interest in protecting and presenting the heritage.

The principal points and conclusions of the group discussions were assembled into a document presented at the closing ceremony in Athens on 12 May, included herein as "Conclusions of the Conference Participants." In it the participants call upon national and international authorities to acknowledge the need to conserve the values of archaeological sites. They recognize the important economic and educational values that sites often have and emphasize the need to manage the conservation of the archaeological heritage, particularly when it is threatened by mass tourism. The participants called specific attention to the important role that management has to play in the articulation of the values that require protection, and they called for the broad participation of interest groups in the formulation of management plans. Finally, participants identified the need to create positions for site managers, to define their roles and responsibilities, and to provide appropriate training for those who are named to such new jobs. Since the conference, these Conclusions have been widely disseminated, both by the Getty organizations and by the individual participants.

About This Publication

Much of the value of the conference was derived from discussions among the participants, from the creation of new networks joining people who share interests and challenges, and from the information that became available from the firsthand viewing of several important sites. It is impossible to convey in a publication the full richness of these experiences. Nevertheless, the organizers hope to further the understanding of the issues related to the conservation of archaeological sites by publishing the presentations as well as by disseminating the views of the organizers and the main points raised in these extraordinary discussions.

The Conclusions are presented first, for they were universally seen as the blueprint for future action. They summarize what the participants identified as the issues central to the preservation of archaeological sites in the Mediterranean today.

The chapter entitled "The Archaeological Heritage in the Mediterranean Region" provides background to the Conclusions by presenting many of the issues taken into consideration in the preparation of the conference, as well as surveying the main points raised in discussions among the participants. The following four presentations on the management, reconstruction, and presentation of archaeological sites set forth the conference's main themes. The introductory lectures on the three sites are included to illustrate, with specific cases, the ideas and problems addressed in the conference.

While not strictly the proceedings of the conference, this publication is intended to convey the substance of the discussions, the concerns of participants, and some recommendations that identify the principal issues and propose possible resolutions. The challenges of conserving the archaeological heritage in the Mediterranean region cannot be properly addressed without a concerted effort involving those individuals who can influence decisions, including the allocation of resources and the proper use of sites. We hope that this publication will help all those who value this heritage as they continue the search for workable solutions that address their particular interests and, most important of all, conserve the diverse values of these remarkable sites, today and for future generations.

Acknowledgments

For a conference lasting only five full days, the list of people who made it possible is long. First, the organizers would like to acknowledge the pivotal role played by the conference participants. From the beginning, they embraced the initiative with enthusiasm and participated in the discussions with open minds and warm collegiality. With good humor and patience, they endured a grueling schedule of presentations, visits, and meetings, as well as many hours aboard the ship and in buses. The conference enjoyed calm seas throughout the five days—the final blessing contributing to the event's success.

During the long months of preparation, the conference organizers relied on the sage advice of an informal advisory group that included Anton Bammer, William D. E. Coulson, Christos Doumas, Hermann Kienast, Helmut Kyrieleis, Marc Laenen, and Vassilis Lambrinoudakis. The preparatory meetings took us to Santorini, Rome, and Athens, where we were hosted respectively by the Idryma Theras P. M. Nomikos Foundation, the Memmo Foundation, and the Archaeology Department of the University of Athens.

The site presentations would not have been possible without the generous collaboration of the authorities and archaeologists at each site. The authors of the site presentations have included their acknowledgments in their articles.

In Tunis we received the support and warm hospitality of the Ministry of Culture of Tunisia; of Abdelaziz Daoulatli, director of the Institut National du Patrimoine; and of Abdel Majid Ennabli, who welcomed us to the Carthage Museum for the opening of the conference. The arrangements for receiving the participants in Tunis were greatly facilitated by our indefatigable friend Aicha Ben Abed.

The speakers set the stage for discussion and raised provocative points. Aicha Ben Abed, Zahi Hawass, Hermann Kienast, Margaret Mac Lean, and Giora Solar presented the values of archaeological sites in a panel on the first day. Aboard ship, Christos Doumas, Hartwig Schmidt, Renée Sivan, and Sharon Sullivan addressed the management and presentation of sites. The introductions to Piazza Armerina, Knossos, and Ephesus were prepared and presented respectively by Nicholas Stanley-Price, John K. Papadopoulos, and Martha Demas. The discussions were led and recorded by Aicha Ben Abed, Brigitte Bourgeois, Christos Doumas,

Vassos Karageorghis, Vassilis Lambrinoudakis, Demetrios Michaelides, and Giora Solar, in collaboration with members of the Getty staff.

Arriving in Athens after four days at sea, the group was welcomed for the closing ceremonies at the Aula Magna of the University of Athens by the rector. The organizers recognize the importance of every single person's contribution, and all have our gratitude and thanks.

The smooth development of our itinerary would not have been possible without the scrupulous attention of Mhairi Forbes and Susan Guerrero to the million and one details required to move a large group smoothly through four countries by various modes of transportation. Phyllis Lapin and Romany Helmy worked with Oscar García, Mario Cabrera, Deak Tinner, and Germán Rodríguez, security officers of the J. Paul Getty Trust, to shepherd us safely through sites, docks, and airports.

Final recognition must go to the Getty staff who worked together for two years to realize this project. The Mediterranean Conference team—Marion True, Margaret Mac Lean, Martha Demas, Jerry Podany, John Papadopoulos, Nicholas Stanley-Price, and Susan Guerrero—were committed collaborators who worked closely with the conference director, Marta de la Torre.

Miguel Angel Corzo
Director
The Getty Conservation Institute

John Walsh
Director
The J. Paul Getty Museum

Conclusions of the Conference Participants

THE INTRINSIC IMPORTANCE and finite nature of archaeological resources have been recognized in various international charters. The participants in this conference support these charters and urge their implementation. In recent years, various forces have increased the threat to these sites: among others, rapidly increasing urbanization, environmental degradation, natural disasters, violent conflicts, and, in many countries, a lack of resources for their maintenance. The extraordinary growth of mass tourism in the last few years has brought about a change in the way archaeological sites are used. Archaeological sites are nonrenewable resources, however, and, as such, must be managed and maintained.

There is now a need to define more fully the values that archaeological sites hold for all humanity, present and future, and to develop processes to manage and present these sites. The conservation of a site's cultural values is the paramount aim of these processes. In the realization that archaeological sites are important economic resources and in view of increasing public interest, an organized approach to decision making would assure the conservation and preservation of the various values of the archaeological sites, including their educational and economic potential.

The participants of the conference on the Conservation of Archaeological Sites in the Mediterranean Region in their discussions came to the following conclusions:

1. Archaeological sites hold values for a variety of groups (archaeologists, tourists, students, national and local communities, and others). These groups value the sites in different ways, and their values have a direct effect on the ultimate fate of the sites.
2. Since decisions taken regarding the different uses of a site affect its values, a systematic and comprehensive approach should be adopted in the process of making decisions about sites.
3. An interdisciplinary group representing the various constituencies of the site should participate directly in the decision-making process. The management process must

begin with thorough research and consultation with all those concerned, leading to a statement of significance of the values of the site, followed by the setting of management policy and strategies for its implementation.

4. This management process should be led by specially designated individuals. Their role and responsibility must be defined according to the needs of each site, as well as to the structures and laws that govern each site.

5. Additional training should be provided for the preparation of specialists (archaeologists, architects, art historians, and others) who might become responsible for the management of sites. Such training should be extended to those already responsible for archaeological sites by means of courses developed by the appropriate international and national organizations acting in concert.

6. The uses of a cultural site often evolve in the course of time. Therefore, the requirements for its management may change accordingly.

7. The director of a proposed excavation should guarantee from the beginning of research the presence of various specialists required for an interdisciplinary approach, and acknowledge in the plan the fair representation of the interests of different constituencies. The granting of permits for excavation should depend on compliance with this requirement as well as with national laws.

8. It is recognized that many archaeological sites can be important economic resources. Mass tourism offers an opportunity to utilize these sites for economic benefit, but at the same time it increases the risk of decay and destruction. The management process should take this into account.

9. Archaeological sites can also be educational resources. Plans for the presentation of such sites should respond to this potential and involve appropriately qualified professionals. Continuing evaluation should be an integral part of these plans.

10. The participants recommend that governments and other national and international agencies recognize and support this new concept of sites and their management.

Athens, 12 May 1995

PART ONE

The Management and Presentation of Archaeological Sites

Introduction to Part One

THE MANAGEMENT and presentation of archaeological sites are topics of great scope and complexity. Each, indeed, could be the subject of a specialized publication. The first piece, by Marta de la Torre and Margaret Mac Lean, presents an overview of the issues addressed by the conference. The other four papers consider various specific issues in more detail: two deal with the process of managing archaeological sites, and two with methods of presentation. These topics were selected in order to give participants the opportunity to hear the views of several specialists on issues relevant to the discussions held during the conference. These papers, revised and expanded, along with the general overview, are published in the following pages.

The essay by Marta de la Torre and Margaret Mac Lean discusses the diverse threats to the archaeological heritage and presents the wide range of values—educational, economic, and historical—ascribed to complex heritage sites. It also addresses, in general terms, the need to balance the interests of protection and visitation.

Sharon Sullivan's paper explains the planning process that has been developed in Australia for the management of cultural sites. In the context of plans developed by this process, the stated aim of the management of a cultural site is to conserve the values that constitute each site's significance. Sullivan presents the various steps required for the preparation of these plans; while emphasizing that successful plans must be appropriate to the particular situation of each site, she formulates principles that are relevant to cultural sites in general.

A site on the Greek island of Thera is presented to illustrate the application of the process presented by Sullivan to a site in the Mediterranean region. Focusing on the site of Akrotiri, where he has worked as an archaeologist for many years, Christos Doumas analyzes its significance and explains the management decisions that have been made there in recent years to protect the site and open it to visitors.

The contributions of Hartwig Schmidt and Renée Sivan, meanwhile, illustrate two views concerning the presentation of sites. Schmidt focuses on the reconstruction of historical structures, an approach that in the past has been used widely in the Mediterranean, and discusses its effects on the authenticity and values of sites. Sivan, a member of the new professional group of presentation specialists, discusses the use of interpretation techniques borrowed from such fields as education and entertainment. Some of these techniques have been introduced only recently into the archaeological world and are the subject of much debate as to the appropriateness of their use in cultural sites. This new exploration of site interpretation and presentation constitutes an emerging area of heritage work, and, like any nascent discipline, its parameters and guiding principles are still being explored.

The topic of site interpretation and presentation was included in the conference and in this volume because, regardless of the methods used, the ways in which a site is presented and interpreted can affect the integrity of its values and, thus, its conservation as well.

The Archaeological Heritage in the Mediterranean Region

Marta de la Torre and Margaret Mac Lean

A S WE BUILD what will one day become the remains of our society, we destroy what has come down to us from earlier times. The surviving remains of the past are finite and vulnerable. The Mediterranean region contains the vestiges of the ancient civilizations that shaped our own societies. If these are destroyed—whether by overuse, neglect, or failed intervention—the tangible evidence of the past will be erased for future generations.

Once it is destroyed or its authenticity compromised, the archaeo-logical heritage cannot be reinstated. The only way to ensure its survival is to devise and employ ways of caring for heritage sites which do not deplete them. These sites must be managed and used carefully, for as unique, nonrenewable resources, they will inevitably be consumed if exploited without long-term plans. Unfortunately, few long-term conserva-tion plans can be found today in the Mediterranean region—a situation that is leading to the irreversible degradation of the physical fabric and the cultural value of many archaeological sites.

After their initial abandonment, it was common for architectural remains to be ignored by subsequent generations who lived and died around them. In many places, the only interest the ruins held for local populations was their use as sources of building materials or as corrals for animals.

In the early nineteenth century, a few travelers in search of romance and adventure visited the overgrown remains of past civilizations. Later, as scholars and scientists studied the sites and shaped our knowledge and understanding about the people who created them, the places attracted the increasing interest of the public. Today, archaeological sites in the Mediterranean region are the destinations of millions of visitors every year.

These sites have come to be valued by many elements of society for a variety of reasons. For scholars they are the subjects of study and provide the bases of their academic advancement and reputation. Nations and regions anchor their national or ethnic identities in their interpreta-tion of the archaeological record. Certain regions owe their economic well-being to the presence of a popular site. Many countries exploit them successfully as sources of foreign currency, through their appeal for tourism—the largest industry in the world.

Paradoxically, as the values of archaeological sites are recognized by those who have a stake in them, the rate of destruction increases. Unplanned and unchecked development compromises many sites; new infrastructures and environmental changes alter the conditions that preserved them in the past. Excessive and unmanaged visitation, often coupled with inappropriate interventions that attempt to "preserve" the new tourist attractions, can destroy exactly what visitors want to experience.

Threats to the Archaeological Heritage

The factors that threaten the survival of the Mediterranean archaeological heritage are complex and varied. Normal population growth and its accompanying infrastructure can encroach upon a site and damage it permanently, occasionally without the surrounding community even taking notice. In some places, the archaeological remains foster growth by attracting visitors and, along with them, people who come to pursue economic opportunities created by the new demand for services.

Ancient populations settled in locations that were and continue to be highly desirable—coastal regions, fertile valleys, and high vantage points. Because contemporary landowners seek the same agreeable environments, there is often strong demand for lands around heritage sites not yet protected by legislation. The rise in market value of these lands can drive the original populations away or make it more expensive for authorities to expropriate land for archaeological protection.

These changes can bring with them radical transformations in the use of the land surrounding archaeological sites. Many archaeology-rich regions in the Mediterranean, where just a decade ago the land was dedicated mainly to agriculture, have been converted today into resort communities with a profusion of high-rise hotels, restaurants, and commercial enterprises catering to the tourist trade. This kind of development brings with it the creation and enhancement of service infrastructures. Construction of roads and highways facilitates tourism and communications; and better electrical, water, and sewer systems make life healthier and more comfortable for local inhabitants. Without doubt these factors improve the economic condition of the population, but they can create serious threats to the archaeological record by massively changing the environment in which it survived for centuries. The pernicious effect of these sorts of environmental changes can take years to become evident.

More immediately visible destruction is created by other factors, such as natural catastrophes and violent conflict. Sadly, in recent years, there have been too many examples of the consequences that warfare can have on the cultural heritage.

The most commonly cited reason for deterioration is the lack of human and financial resources available for site conservation and maintenance; this problem is exacerbated by increased numbers of visitors. The income from admission receipts very often goes into general accounts in heritage agencies or into national treasuries, and allocation of resources to individual sites that generated this income seldom seems to be based on their actual maintenance and conservation requirements.

As countries around the Mediterranean come to depend increasingly on income from tourism, archaeologists and cultural authorities are encouraged to make their sites more attractive to visitors. This can lead to the reconstruction of architectural elements, the use of ancient structures for cultural events, and the proliferation of services for visitors. Presentation and use of the site and development of tourism infrastructure can be legitimate endeavors that enhance the values of a site. Yet these activities can also destroy the values if they are implemented without planning and coordination.

In recent decades these sites have come to be viewed as the common heritage of humanity, and it is accepted that they should be accessible to visitors from around the world. Yet the responsibility for protection of sites falls on the individual countries in which they are located. Uncoordinated management of sites and monuments as well as problems of damage and deterioration caused by large numbers of visitors are common everywhere. Participants in the conference considered that in many cases damage from the lack of management and maintenance could be mitigated through practical collaborations among those who have a stake in the survival of these resources—including cultural officials, international and private organizations, and commercial tourism organizations. The Conclusions that were issued at the end of the conference reflect these beliefs.

Importance of Sites

The values perceived in the archaeological heritage by various segments of society depend on the many different qualities and meanings that they ascribe to these sites. These interest groups do not cherish the same things, and their perceptions of what is important about a site are very often in conflict. Those who have the task of administering the archaeological heritage must ensure that these places are used by society in ways that do not sacrifice the elements that make the sites significant. This requirement is the most difficult challenge facing stewards of the heritage.

In order to care effectively for a place, one must see clearly the things about it that are important and worth protecting as well as the risks that threaten it. To achieve this requires a plan built on answers to some basic questions: What constitutes an archaeological site? What are its features? What is important about it? What threatens these aspects? Who considers its features and history significant? What are the value or values they perceive in it?

Central here is the importance of the articulation of these values. Because they are so profoundly subjective, values are best expressed by someone who believes in them. With this premise in mind, one can consider the values vested in archaeological sites in the Mediterranean region, the features in which those values might be embodied, and the people who cherish the sites.

Value can be understood more clearly if some of the possible meanings of the word in this context are enumerated. Value can be equated with *usefulness* if the place can be used for productive purposes, such as the education of citizens; or with *significance,* if the place signifies or symbolizes something larger and more important than merely the ruins of its architecture. The current benefit can be understood as the positive effects on the community, culture, national image, and so forth, that derive from the existence of the place. The potential can be understood as the possibility of further scientific information or other benefits that the place is perceived to be able to yield. Both benefit and potential constitute value.

A cultural heritage site can have many different values: aesthetic, historical, social, scientific, religious, economic, educational, and so on.

If a place is seen by a stakeholder as having *scientific value,* it might be useful or significant now or in the future for the archaeological community. This judgment might be made because the site holds important evidence for some newly understood feature of ancient culture and has not yet been excavated and thus not yet damaged. As was noted above, certain threats can ultimately destroy these values. One way in which scientific value could be compromised, for example, would be if a new visitors center were built on top of a site before archaeologists were able to understand the place through excavation and protection of its unique evidence. Conversely, the *educational value* of the same place would be compromised if archaeologists were allowed to excavate so much of the site that nothing would remain of its features for interpretation to the public.

Its *aesthetic value* could be endangered if, for example, new constructions were to obstruct the ancient view of a mountain in the distance—part of the meaning and beauty of the site.

Archaeological sites are valuable to segments of society for various reasons, and aspects of the sites are variably significant. If one group's interests are allowed to take precedence over the interests of others, values important to many will be sacrificed. Ideally, a well-balanced approach to managing a site protects the separate values and educates stakeholders about the values important to others.

Articulation and recognition of a particular set of values for a site is only the first step necessary to ensure their protection. Any threats to those values must be understood, and a plan must be devised to anticipate and mitigate them.

In some cases, aspects of a site must be developed in order to reveal their full significance. For example, a visitor might find educational value in the story told by the place—but only if the story is made legible. A tour organizer may find the place valuable because of its location—but only if there are adequate roads to reach it and sufficient amenities to accommodate several busloads of visitors per day. In purely economic terms, the size of the site, old trees around the perimeter that allow respite from the sun, and the view all encourage an extended stay and enhance opportunities for sales of food and souvenirs and even for overnight accommodations. These opportunities translate into value for the tourism industry.

In many instances, the difference in reasons that a site is valued by certain groups generates conflict. For example, an important archaeological site might stand near what has become a popular bathing resort, and developers want to build a hotel there, taking advantage of the site's attraction for visitors. However, the presence of the hotel might damage the view, introduce many more people into a fragile area, lead to the need for new subterranean pipes and other services, and require changes in the route into the site. Complete destruction of the site and its significance can take place if all these changes are made without an understanding of their impact on the site, and in the absence of sufficient resources for site management and protection. In situations that embody such conflicts, a process that can guide management decisions is potentially highly useful. (An example of such a process is found in Sullivan, herein.)

Educational Value of Sites

Because learning can occur on many levels, the educational value of sites is appreciated by many groups; thus, educational value is the common ground among most of the constituencies. A site can provide lessons in history, cultural expression, art, architecture, societal development, and conflict, and such lessons can benefit the specialist archaeologists, the tourism officials, the general public, and even the developers. In previous eras, excavations were undertaken in a search for treasures to fill museums in distant lands. Now, however, the purpose of most archaeological inquiry is to develop reasonable and well-supported answers to significant hypotheses. Archaeology as a discipline intends to read the full range of evidence from a site (objects, context, architecture, and so on) and then to use the discoveries to further knowledge that can or must be used to interpret the site for the public. Unfortunately, even these new approaches to archaeology do not necessarily result in a site that is understandable to the public. Since society supports and funds academic archaeology, it would be logical to require that scholars include in the excavation planning process other specialists who can consider the future presentation of the site to visitors.

Throughout most of the world, the interpretation and presentation of archaeological sites to the public are woefully underdeveloped both in theory and in practice. Sites without information for visitors are not easily understood by nonspecialists—and without some explanation even specialists can be challenged to understand, for example, an overgrown trench or protruding wall foundations. Moreover, archaeologists are not yet helpful in site presentation, since their training rarely encourages them to speak to the general public. Nevertheless, good interpretation enables visitors to understand archaeology and can convert them from puzzled tourists into advocates for archaeological research and conservation.

Interpretation and presentation must be viewed and accepted as obligations to the visitor—not only as means of attracting more tourists.

In recent years, some countries around the Mediterranean have begun to use funds derived from tourism for the study, conservation, and presentation of heritage sites. While some interesting (albeit controversial) interpretation experiments are being undertaken in the Mediterranean (see Sivan, herein), far more attention could usefully be spent in this area. Cost-effective approaches, innovative methods, and planning techniques are being tested and evaluated; the dissemination of the results of such experiments would be an important contribution to everyone in the field.

Guidebooks available on site—particularly at the larger sites—are useful. Well-informed guides are often excellent diplomats who represent the site, the importance of protecting it, the discipline of archaeology itself, and the host country. Interpretive panels in strategic areas can guide visitors toward areas safe for walking and away from fragile areas. In some cases, restoration of a feature of a site can help visitors visualize the original nature, scale, beauty, or arrangement of a place.

There are international conventions designed to guide the work of archaeological restoration (see Appendix A). When implemented appropriately and explained effectively to the visitor, restoration can be an important educational tool (see Schmidt, herein). For the majority of cases, however, reconstruction is not appropriate; instead, models or drawings can show the site in its original configuration and in relation to other such places regionally. In contrast to reconstruction, such models can also be easily changed to reflect recent research findings.

Visitors can benefit from exposure to books, guides, panels, or models that create a context for their experience at the site; inform them about its features, history, and significance; and advise them about what to expect on the tour. Good interpretation not only enhances the educational value of the site but also has many other salutary effects on visitors. Informed visitors are far more likely to avoid damaging a site, for they can quickly develop a protective attitude about a place that means something to them. Good interpretation, however, requires thought and planning, which must start during the initial phases of excavation.

Archaeological Heritage as an Economic Resource

Both natural and cultural sites have become important economic resources in many parts of the world, and their economic potential is almost always realized through tourism. While the degradation of both natural and cultural resources in the presence of large numbers of visitors is inevitable when the situation is unmanaged, there is a stronger awareness of the dangers that affect the natural habitat than of those that imperil archaeological sites. The conservation of the values of such natural sites as beaches, forests, and landscapes is known to be closely tied to their long-term economic value. There are many examples on the Mediterranean coast of dirty, overcrowded, overbuilt beach resorts that now attract fewer tourists or attract a less desirable class of tourism that brings fewer economic benefits. The erosion of the integrity of these natural sites has eroded their commercial value as well.

This phenomenon does not seem to be recognized in the case of archaeological sites, however—perhaps because of critical differences in visitors' perception of value. While everyone prefers a beach with uncluttered space, clean sand, and clear water, many visitors appear not to mind a crowded, unmaintained, or erroneously reconstructed archaeological site.

In fact, many overcrowded sites that provide tourists with a visit of less than optimal quality seem to attract larger numbers of visitors every year. It appears that if a site attracts large crowds, it becomes a must-see for all tour organizers, who promote an even greater influx of tourists. While one site receives visitors by busloads, other nearby sites remain almost deserted. Vivid examples of this type of disparity are found throughout the Mediterranean region, as on the western coast of Turkey, where Ephesus receives over a million and a half visitors every year while Priene, Miletus, and Dydima are visited by only a fraction of this number.

Lack of communication between the tourism industry and the cultural sector seems to be the cause of many of these imbalances. Yet an even more serious problem is that in many countries, the national agencies in charge of tourism development and those responsible for the cultural heritage pursue their objectives entirely independently; this disjunction often creates serious conflicts whose results are evident worldwide.

Cultural heritage professionals have started to advocate a more coordinated and thoughtful approach to archaeological resource management. It is now recognized that sites have a maximum carrying capacity that cannot be exceeded without serious consequences. These consequences have an impact on the site itself but can also affect visitors. Site managers have attempted to impose limitations on the number of people who can be in a site at a given time—but they have been unable to do so without immediately feeling the pressure of other interests.

The use of ancient monuments for entertainment and social events brings additional income to local populations and authorities. In many cases, however, ancient structures have lost the structural integrity required to provide safe accommodations to crowds. In such instances, not only is the monument endangered; the public is endangered as well.

When visiting archaeological sites, tourists entrust their safety to tour operators, and cultural authorities make little effort to influence the potentially hazardous flow of visitors. There is little doubt that some powerful groups who value archaeological sites do so mainly for their economic potential. A disturbing trend in recent decades has been the high priority placed on economic value while all other values are ignored.

Very few studies have been done in the areas of site management and the economics of conservation—whether on the subject of the relationship of visitors and deterioration, the impact of a deteriorated site on visitor interest, or the appropriate allocation of national budgets to various archaeological sites. Nevertheless, there is an increased awareness of the need to conserve the "goose that lays the golden egg." This awareness must be accompanied by research and study to further understanding of the dynamics of managing these irreplaceable resources.

Balancing the Interests of Protection and Visitation

It is not universally recognized that archaeological sites have legitimate value to many groups and that the views of these constituents should be considered in decisions that affect the sites. This situation is evidenced by the fact that decisions continue to be made unilaterally based on the interest of particular groups.

Archaeologists continue to excavate without providing for the conservation of their discoveries or for the presentation and interpretation of the site to the public; national authorities decide to promote a site without consulting with the local population; tourism operators include sites in their tours without considering the impact of the larger number of visitors; dams are built without any study of their effect on the water table below the archaeological sites; hotels spring up around sites, and their water and waste disposal contaminates and decays the archaeological remains. The list is long, and little seems to be learned from tragic examples.

While not all conflicts can be solved to everyone's satisfaction, much could be advanced by a coherent planning process involving broad consultation of concerned groups.

As is well recognized in the field of management, there is no one right formula applicable to all situations. This is true also of the archaeological heritage, where there are many variances, from site to site and from country to country, in the values, administrative environment, threats to sites, condition of the remains, numbers of visitors, and available resources. These differences do not mean that there are no solutions but, rather, that specific solutions must be found for each site. For cultural heritage professionals, however, there can be only one objective in the management of an archaeological site, and that is to conserve its values. This determination of the values that take priority at a given site must be made in consultation with all stakeholders, and it must reflect a long-term view of the site and its use.

Many countries and international organizations have developed management approaches to cultural heritage which vary in their effectiveness. One of the most successful models, employed in Australia and embodied in the Australian ICOMOS *Burra Charter,* is presented in this volume (see Sullivan and Appendix A, herein). Successful cultural management starts with a planning process that results in a management plan to guide all major policy decisions as well as day-to-day operations at a site.

A management plan will not provide answers to every question that might emerge in the future. Rather, its usefulness lies in articulating policies for different areas of activities—such as excavation, conservation, visitor management, interpretation, and maintenance—that are in accordance with the significance of the site and with the values to be conserved. These policies will provide the framework for decisions that must be made, now and in the future, in each of these areas.

In addition, because the creation of a management plan relies on collaboration and communication among the various interest groups, its benefits are derived as much from the consultative process as from the resulting written document.

Questions that are much discussed during initial phases of the process proposed here are Who should lead the design of the plan? and Who should guide its implementation? These are two distinct procedures. The first is the process of bringing the stakeholders together, articulating the values they perceive in the site, describing the goals for the plan, and so on, through the several steps of eliciting and organizing information; the result is a written management plan. The second process is the day-to-day management of the site, which involves the making of decisions in accordance with the various strategies that are devised for visitor management, physical protection, condition monitoring, maintenance, and ongoing evaluation.

Archaeologists with official permission to investigate a site have as their primary interest the building of intellectual theories to explain the physical features that are revealed. Traditionally, while these experts are the most knowledgeable about a site's scientific significance, they might not know much at all about how to protect the site—from visitors or from simple exposure—or how to tell the story of the site in terms accessible to the general public. Interestingly, archaeologists have also traditionally been impatient with the idea of welcoming the public into "their" sites, since they can often see the visitor as a distraction and a liability. It seems reasonable, therefore, to consider the site archaeologist as an important member of the group involved in creating a plan, not as the only person who should be consulted.

The role of the site manager is to ensure the implementation of the plan as developed by the larger group, including protection of the values identified by the stakeholders. The site manager assumes the responsibility of operational decisions that follow the policies set out for the site. For certain aspects of operations, the site manager calls on other individuals with specialized skills. A site manager cannot work independently, and a major part of the day-to-day implementation work is to maintain coordination with national and local authorities, as well as with other groups who have access to and use of the site.

Experience in some parts of the world shows that the responsibilities of managing a site can be effectively assumed by individuals with various professional backgrounds, including archaeology, architecture, and conservation. Site managers should have an interest in managing as well as the necessary skills to do so. These qualifications are more important than having a background in a particular profession.

New managerial positions will need to be created, and, in almost all cases, these individuals will need to be trained in new skills. In the future, such management skills will become part of the education of professionals likely to be responsible for heritage sites. Until such a time, managers could be trained through specially designed short courses organized at the national or regional level.

Site management, as defined and advocated in this volume, constitutes a new approach to the care of sites in the Mediterranean region. If it is to be adopted successfully, the decision-making process must be evaluated. Successful implementation of this approach will require coordinated management at the level of the national authorities, as well as the education of the various groups with vested interests in the archaeological heritage.

At this time, there seems to be little regional experience in managing sites for the purpose of their long-term protection. While it can be seen that some sites have been conserved with more success than others, there is almost no information about the processes that were followed or the decisions that were made. Research and dissemination of cases that can be used as examples of the successful application of well-designed, long-term strategies would be highly useful to those interested in introducing new approaches to managing sites in the Mediterranean region.

Open, negotiated management is new to many places and is often rejected a priori as impracticable or as "not feasible" in certain cultures. The shift toward a participatory process of systematic decision making is never a simple step. In most cases, agencies or interest groups need to relinquish a degree of authority to which they have been accustomed or entitled. The Mediterranean region has a long history of excavation and tourism at archaeological sites; in some cases, the administrative structures for cultural heritage have been in place for generations and are resistant to change. The implementation of inclusive management approaches can take place only if policy makers see potential advantages in such a change and if resources are allocated to put them into place. While the conference participants recognized that it is difficult to make decisions that introduce radical change, they encouraged national authorities to adopt comprehensive approaches to site management to assure significant, long-term benefits for the conservation of the archaeological heritage of the Mediterranean region.

A Planning Model for the Management of Archaeological Sites

Sharon Sullivan

THE CONSERVATION OF A CULTURAL SITE can be achieved only through a comprehensive approach to management that takes into consideration all of the site's values. Conservation decisions are most effective when they are based on the information gathered during a formal planning process designed to identify appropriate management practices and actions.

Over the years cultural heritage professionals have put forth a number of conservation principles intended to guide their work. These principles and practices have taken the form of international charters and recommendations (see Appendix A). The most famous of these is *The Venice Charter,* adopted by the International Council of Monuments and Sites (ICOMOS) in 1965.

In 1988 Australia ICOMOS adapted the principles of *The Venice Charter* to local conditions and put them forth as *The Burra Charter.* The principles of *The Burra Charter* have been used to devise a planning method that has dramatically improved the management of sites, as well as their ongoing conservation. This method has been adapted successfully for use in the United States and in China. The process of adaptation of the method is essential, since management approaches must be suited to local conditions and traditions, including the social, economic, political, and physical environments.

The planning method described in this article consists of a series of interrelated steps, undertaken in a logical order and resulting in a management plan for the site. It provides a structure for approaching a complex situation and for designing appropriate solutions intended to conserve the site's cultural significance. Planning requires an investment of both time and resources, and it is important to complete the process in its logical order to lay the foundation for success in the management of the site. The information presented here provides only the skeletal structure and guidelines for the process. For them to result in a useful management plan, they must be developed with information related to the site under consideration.

The principal objective of a management plan is to conserve the cultural significance of a site, not to meet the needs of tourists, archaeologists, or developers—although these concerns may also be addressed to varying degrees. A site's cultural significance is determined by the values society perceives either in it or in elements of it. The value can be aesthetic, scientific, historic, or social, or a combination of these. Other values—especially financial and educational—are sometimes considered as well. Financial and educational values are very real, but derive essentially from aspects of cultural significance: they exist only as long as the cultural significance exists.

Identifying all the values of a place, bringing together the individuals who can influence decisions that affect the site, and obtaining a clear understanding of the management realities are critical steps of the planning process. The information thus obtained is essential for the design of realistic and workable management strategies.

Why a Management Plan?

It is often asked whether a formal planning process is really necessary. Most individuals working in the cultural field are committed to the conservation of sites and recognize that they have cultural value, and many of these sites are already designated as important national- or world-heritage resources. Almost everyone, including the public, wishes to see the places preserved. Why, then, is formal planning necessary? Many managers object when asked to prepare such a plan, and they object even more when "foreign" experts are invited to do this work. They believe that they know the site, its values, and its problems, and that going through a formal planning process is a waste of time and money. They have an important point. Considerable resources and foreign expertise have been invested in planning exercises that result in plans that are technically impractical, that are impossibly costly, or that do not elicit enough political support to ensure implementation. Managers generally feel the need to press on with immediate solutions to what they see as urgent problems. However, this unplanned approach leads to ad hoc decisions that can result in unanticipated, negative consequences in the short and long terms.

Decisions made without a plan can be counterproductive and often dangerous. Serious conflict can arise from a lack of understanding of certain values of a site or of the management dynamics at work there. Other problems can arise from the exclusion from the planning process of a key discipline or area of expertise, or an important group or individual who can influence the future of a site. Unnecessary damage can result when the logical sequence of management steps is disregarded, as in the case where a site is excavated without any provision or plan for its conservation and future management.

Figure 1 presents the sequence of steps required to prepare a management plan. The goal of such plans is always to protect and conserve the cultural significance of the sites through appropriate management decisions. The plan is intended to put in place a range of protective actions that prevent or slow the deterioration of the site, whether that deterioration is physical or, rather, relates to the loss of other cultural values.

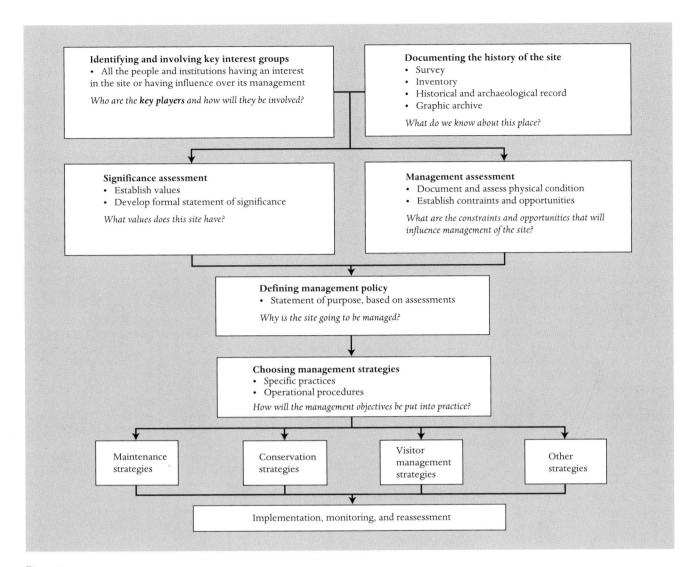

Figure 1
The planning process.

Identifying and Involving Key Interest Groups

We can borrow from folklore to make a crucial point. Most cultures have a version of the story of the "bad fairy." A European version is told in "Sleeping Beauty," in which a king and queen long for a child and, finally, hoping against hope, have a beautiful daughter. To celebrate her birth, they invite the richest, best-dressed, and most influential fairies of the kingdom, expecting that their guests will become the child's godmothers and bestow valuable gifts on the infant. These fairies are indeed generous, conferring upon the child beauty, goodness, wisdom, the ability to attract foreign currency, and so on. The princess's future looks very bright. Whether deliberately or as an oversight, however, the king and queen do not invite one difficult but powerful fairy to the celebrations. She arrives anyway: late, badly dressed (spoiling the decor), and in a very bad temper, upsetting the carefully planned event. She does not bestow any gifts on the beautiful princess; instead, she puts a curse on her and causes endless trouble in the kingdom. Eventually, as a result, the princess falls asleep for one hundred years, and the kingdom falls into ruin.

The moral we can learn from this story is that any plans for the future of a cultural site will not work unless all the key players are involved in the conceptualization of the plan and feel that they participate in the ownership of the proposed outcomes. The key players are those for whom the site has value, those who have important information about it, and those who can influence its management. These constituents will vary from place to place and from country to country. In most instances the managers of sites—be they archaeologists, architects, or civil servants—regard themselves as the only key players. But a thorough analysis of interest groups can identify people from city governments, tourist authorities, local communities, and tour organizations, as well as foreign and local scholars and other experts such as conservators, who may have a crucial role to play in the development of effective management for a site.

The first task of the planning process is to identify representatives of all the key interest groups, bring them together, and hear their concerns. This is an essential step, as well as an ongoing element, that will broaden understanding of the value of the place, as well as of opportunities and constraints. This step can also win new friends and supporters (some in unlikely places) for the conservation of the site. When the key players are involved, or at least satisfied, with the plan's objectives, the likelihood of its successful implementation will increase.

At the core of this group of key players is the person or group responsible for the overall, long-term management of the site.[1] This person or group also pulls together all of these elements and writes the plan. It is the job of this individual or group to guide the planning process—identifying the key players, gathering them at crucial times, and establishing the statement of significance and the management strategies. It will subsequently be the responsibility of the site manager to implement the plan.

Documenting the History of the Site

Concurrently with their identification of key players, those leading the planning process must identify, locate, and document all the background information about the site, such as its history, condition, research, and documentation. This task can include research into the site's history, interviews with local inhabitants, and the commissioning of an overview of the site's archaeological history. The regional and cultural contexts should also be defined. It is important to know not only the details about the site but also how it relates to other sites in the region and what role it plays in the region's history.

Certain sites have an overwhelming quantity of documentary and historical material. In such instances, the information must be summarized and refined, to highlight and put in context the key developments at the site. Where there is information about the research and conservation work on the site, it can be used to reconstruct the intervention history and to explain the site's current condition and configuration.

The process of gathering this documentation will inevitably bring to light gaps in the knowledge about a site—and hence point the way to further necessary research. Often the process can reveal surprising things about a site's history and condition. The articles on Piazza Armerina, Knossos, and Ephesus in this volume illustrate the sort of research that can so usefully inform this process.

Significance Assessment

The significance of a site is usually multifaceted, and any management plan must consider all values and resolve potential conflicts between them. An objective and clear statement of all the reasons a place is important is a central element of any management plan. It assists in the development of management strategies that will safeguard the full significance of the site. These statements are most crucial for very important sites, which tend to have the most interventionist management.

Managers are often skeptical of the necessity of assessing significance—since the values of many sites are believed to be self-evident. Managers or persons in charge generally feel they know the values of an important site. Managers, particularly those with academic backgrounds, tend to focus on the scientific, artistic, and historical values. Even so, a close examination of the complete significance of a site can bring to light other values of importance to different groups.

Some of the categories used to describe the significance of a site are aesthetic, social, scientific, historic, or other special value. A significance assessment should involve a careful analysis of all these values. It can be useful to consider refining the definitions, as well as using subsets under principal values. For instance, educational value, or value to a particular group of people, could be seen as subsets of social value. A place that demonstrates changes in technology, style, or use over time through the accretions it has acquired may have historic as well as aesthetic value. And in such a case, the historical value may be in conflict to some extent with the aesthetic or architectural value—that is, the accretions may demonstrate the rich history of the site, but the removal of those accretions may reveal more fully the original beauty of the design. Conversely, reconstruction of a ruin may reinstate the site's original beauty but diminish its value for scientific or archaeological research.

Once recognized, the values of a site may sometimes be seen to conflict with one another. More often than not, however, wise management can achieve a balanced protection of the values. On the rare occasions when it seems necessary to sacrifice aspects of one value to conserve another, it is crucial first to explore thoroughly all the facets of the values and to consider a range of alternative management strategies.

Thus, significance assessment is essential because, even when a site is considered to be of Unesco World Heritage status—very important, legally protected, and proposed for active conservation—managers need detail as to why it is significant in order to protect the values that make it so. In fact, the greater the level of physical intervention envisioned, the more detailed the assessment of significance or value should be, since the possibility of damaging or destroying undetected or poorly understood aspects of significance is much more likely as intervention increases.

Even in sites that are recognized as having universal "cultural" value, there are conflicts that must be resolved through management decisions. In the Mediterranean region, evidence of a conflict resides in the use of the term *archaeological* to describe ancient sites. These sites have been found and/or understood through archaeological exploration and research, and their value is revealed by the archaeologists who can interpret the results. However, the actual value of such sites is not, in fact, archaeological; archaeology is simply the means whereby their scientific value and thus their cultural value have been manifested. There are broader cultural values that constitute the most important, overarching significance of these sites—informational or research value is only one. These include their social value as a source of pride to the peoples of the region, and their value as an educational tool for them and for other visitors. They also include their value as historical markers, as well as their important symbolic significance. It might be more appropriate to call them *heritage* sites rather than archaeological sites and to manage them for the conservation of all these values.

Archaeological or research value can sometimes be in conflict with the site's social or public value. Opening a site to public visitation indiscriminately or carrying out "restoration" for this purpose without archaeological investigation can certainly compromise the important scientific potential of the site. Conversely, archaeological investigation for "scientific" reasons can expose fragile, beautiful, and historically important remains that are then subject to rapid deterioration. (Alas, there are too many well-known examples of this type of loss.) Conflicts often arise, and bad decisions are made, because not all the values of the site have been researched, documented, agreed upon, and used as a basis for management.

Establishing the significance of a site requires thorough research of all elements of the site, including the whole range of physical, documentary, archaeological, traditional, and other evidence on—or associated with—the site. In this process, the involvement of a team of specialists expert in a broad range of disciplines, with the active involvement of the manager and the key players, will elucidate the various aspects of significance. The significance of a site should be established prior to, and independent of, management considerations. Finally, local attitudes toward the site must be well understood, since they are crucial to significance assessment and to management.[2]

Management Assessment

The steps that follow the assessment of significance are those that determine the physical condition of the site and provide an understanding of the management environment. These two elements establish the conditions under which management will operate, and identify the opportunities and constraints that exist. The factors that create the working environment must be considered at this stage of the planning process. These factors are the legal and policy framework governing the site; the allocation of management responsibilities; the financial and other resources available; the physical condition of the site; technical possibilities; the needs and expectations of the community; current and projected patterns of visitor use; and threats to the fabric, ambience, and values.

Planners usually find that useful information results from such an assessment of the physical condition. A careful examination and recording of the condition of a site can afford insight into the causes of deterioration and damage. When this examination reveals the physical conditions to be dangerous, the usual reaction is to leap to solutions (too often drastic and involving high technology) rather than to continue to diagnose and plan. However, previous steps of the planning process would have resulted in a gathering of historic photos of the site showing the physical condition over time. The planning group can use these documents to compare past conditions to current ones. Sometimes, surprisingly, areas believed to be decaying rapidly are found to have changed little, if at all, over the years. In other areas, conditions that are thought to have existed for long periods of time are found to be accelerating or changing drastically. In either case, the planners will obtain a better understanding of the processes of deterioration affecting the sites and be able to identify the elements that require priority attention in the plan. The information gathered at this time and the records of condition will also be used in later planning stages to establish and implement monitoring procedures that must be part of the plan.

Many technically brilliant and meticulously researched plans for physical conservation or ongoing management are never implemented. One common reason for this is that they are often inappropriate for the management environment in which they are supposed to operate. Expensive equipment that cannot be maintained or complex monitoring procedures that require unavailable knowledge or a high level of resources are worse than useless. Such strategies can do permanent harm if they are recommended in place of more reasonable procedures that would be appropriate and sustainable at a given site.

It is, therefore, very important to consider the general management environment: staffing, budget, visitor numbers (present and projected), legal status, technical conditions, neighboring land use, regional and local land use, and so forth. The only plan that will be effective is a plan appropriate to the management environment and one that—just as important—has been devised, or at least enthusiastically accepted, by local management.

At this stage of the planning, it can be highly advisable to hold a workshop or meeting at which representatives of all the key interest groups can come together. They need first to ensure that the statement of all the values of the site is comprehensive; second, they need to have the opportunity to express their views on the crucial management issues. These meetings are often lively and frank, with participants taking what is often their first opportunity to air their views and grievances; typically, they then move on to propose positive suggestions for future management. This colloquy invariably results in the discovery of important management issues and problems that had prior to this point been poorly understood or even ignored.

A useful way of understanding the management environment at the site—a way that is often advocated by management specialists—is to undertake a quick analysis of the strengths and weaknesses, and consequently of the opportunities and threats, of the management environment.[3] By looking in some detail at budgets and staffing, visitor numbers and physical problems, local political support and government policy, the planning group can gain a realistic understanding of the management situation and determine what elements would be reasonable and useful to inscribe in the management plan.

This analysis should help clarify what actions are possible immediately, what might be planned for the future, and what will succeed because of the support of key players. Many plans written by consultants or international experts are sound and provide solutions that are excellent, technically feasible, and logical. However, they are rarely implemented because they are so often culturally or technically inappropriate for the environment under consideration or because they are not understood or supported by the local managers and politicians.

Defining Management Policy

The data on significance, condition, and management environment will be used to formulate the management policy for the site. The management policy of a site determines how the cultural importance of the place, identified by the statement of significance, may best be conserved in the short and long terms, with the particular constraints, problems, opportunities, and circumstances taken into account. The management policy should articulate, in general terms, the principles and guidelines that will guide the use, investigation, interpretation, physical interventions, and mitigation and salvage (if appropriate) at the site; it should address the management structure and the protocol for decision making about new activities at the site; it should also provide for monitoring and review of the plan.

The policy should clearly state the options available and the way in which its implementation will "change the place, including its setting, affect its significance, affect the locality and its amenity, affect the client owner and user, affect others involved" (Australia ICOMOS 1992:78).

It is easy to describe theoretically the requirements of a management or conservation policy. However, achieving a successful and workable policy that will effectively maximize the conservation opportunities for the place is a complex and multifaceted task, one that requires technical expertise, sound judgment, practical common sense, creative and comprehensive thinking, and adaptability. These are skills that the site manager needs or must have available. The policy cannot be achieved by a recipe or simply by hiring an expert. It requires the attention and expertise of the manager and the commitment of the organization or authority that is responsible for the management of the place.

The management policy of cultural sites must always have conservation as its principal, overarching aim. Other objectives—such as increased revenue from tourism or the use of the site for excavation—must be subordinated to this main aim and are acceptable only if compatible with it. In the long term, conservation is the only way of ensuring the continued existence of this nonrenewable resource.

In summary, the management policy should

1. articulate the implications of the statement of significance;
2. be acceptable to the owner/authority who controls the site;
3. pay due attention to the needs and desires of the community, especially to those with a special interest in the site;
4. be financially feasible and economically viable;
5. be technically feasible and appropriate;
6. provide a long-term management framework;
7. be sufficiently flexible to allow review, improvement, and alteration (Pearson and Sullivan 1995:210).

In the course of discussing this policy, or set of objectives, a number of crucial issues for the site will emerge as managers struggle with the question of how to plan to keep the cultural values of the place intact while managing it in a realistic way, in line with the constraints, opportunities, and issues that have been identified earlier in the process.

Some examples of issues that the management policy might have to resolve are

1. whether protecting fragile parts of the site, through the erection of an intrusive structure, is more appropriate and more in keeping with the statement of significance and the management context than leaving them exposed or protecting them less effectively and thereby keeping the setting and aesthetic feeling of the site more intact;
2. whether access should be allowed to a fragile part of the site that is of great interest to visitors, or be prohibited to prevent damage;
3. what are the best methods to interpret the site—signs, brochures, a visitor center, guided tours, or a combination of these—in keeping with the aesthetic and social values;
4. whether the natural vegetation should be left, removed, or restored—a decision that depends on its importance and its effect on other significant elements of the site;
5. whether research, including excavation, will be allowed on the site and, if so, where, by whom, and under what conditions;
6. what staff is needed at the site (are guides, guards, scientists, or managers the most important components?);
7. what is the best management structure.

Policies that have addressed all the issues important to a site should be discussed, checked against the statement of significance, and written down. These constitute the site management policy.

Choosing Management Strategies

The next stage of the plan is the development of management strategies—that is, the actual steps by which the management policy is implemented. The diagram in Figure 1 places special emphasis on maintenance, conservation, and visitor management strategies as often being the most fundamental and useful, as well as having the most profound effect—for good or ill—depending on their suitability and effectiveness.

Often the development of maintenance and visitor management strategies demonstrates most dramatically the effect that management can have on site preservation with relatively simple practices. Basic maintenance measures—such as clearing vegetation and supervising workers on site—can emerge as equally important for preservation as some of the more elaborate and costly proposals for physical conservation.

This point can be even more dramatically demonstrated when discussed in relation to visitor management. The effect of poorly behaved visitors can be catastrophic in just a short time. Simple observation of the visitors can elucidate patterns of behavior. Who has not observed visitors casually roaming through sites who, when they thought they were unobserved, climbed on walls, posed for pictures on sculpture, picked up loose mosaic tesserae as souvenirs, or carved their names in the stones? The undisputed fact is that ill-behaved visitors can do more damage to a site in one afternoon than will take place in ten or even a hundred years of natural weathering.

These and many other visitor management problems are easy to resolve. They simply require systematic observation by managers and the consequent application of suitable management measures. The possible solutions are relatively simple and inexpensive, and they do not involve high technology. Yet the impact in terms of preventive care and of long-term preservation of the site is impressive. Similarly, observation of visitor flow patterns can result in a greatly enhanced design for a system of visitor management.

Consideration of physical interventions—stabilization, anastylosis, restoration, or reconstruction—is central to the management strategies. As the options are considered within the framework of management planning, a few general principles should be kept in mind:

1. Any intervention must be consistent with the significance of the place and its management policy. Intervention for the sake of appearing to "do something" can be very dangerous and can, in fact, destroy one or all of the values of the site. This situation is perhaps especially likely when conjecture is used as the basis for restoration or reconstruction, or when restoration processes destroy other important values (archaeological value, for example).

2. Physical interventions are often experimental, with disastrous long-term consequences, especially if the solution demands overly elaborate maintenance and monitoring practices that require skills or tools that are not available locally or that cannot be guaranteed over the long term.

3. Physical conservation solutions need to be approached with care and, indeed, with suspicion in most cases. The rule of thumb is that the best solution is the least possible intervention.

Although this article does not deal with them in detail, there are other management strategies that may be relevant at particular sites and therefore must be designed as well. These include

1. in-depth exploration of aspects of significance and condition not covered fully during the initial phases;
2. maintenance and updating of records;
3. appropriate physical conservation strategy;
4. maintenance and protection of physical fabric;
5. control of encroaching development or potentially conflicting management practices;
6. control of research, including the establishment of policy regarding research activities (i.e., excavation) that will be allowed on site (this policy should be in accordance with the conservation policy and should ensure that the significant values of the place are not damaged);
7. visitor use and interpretation;
8. infrastructure development both on site and external to the site, if external development affects the values of the site;
9. curation and conservation of movable artifacts;
10. ongoing consultation with or involvement of particular relevant groups (Pearson and Sullivan 1995:211–12).

Conclusions

Much of site management is simple common sense. The real value of the planning process presented here is that it can be used to pull together, strengthen, and add to local planning principles and practices. The outline of steps must be used and adapted by local planners who have the required background, information, and expertise.

Management planning need not be a long, involved process expected to solve all the major problems of a site at once. The level of planning should fit the capability of the site managers to work through the issues with key stakeholders and to implement realistic solutions. Planning should move in small, discernible steps from the known situation to an improved one.

Although planning and management can be a big undertaking and involve an intensive use of resources, it need not be so. The collaborative method described in this article—by which the basic values, issues, and solutions are drawn from the key players—can be both inexpensive and effective, if given careful attention and planning.

Management planning must be carried out by local groups rather than by external experts, although such experts may facilitate the process. It is the local planner who has the expertise and ability to involve key interest groups.

Because management policy must involve all key interest groups to be effective, it follows that there may be some compromise and some apparently imperfect or incomplete solutions with this method. It also follows that without this involvement, the most technically and ideologically perfect plan may not be implemented. It is the responsibility of the plan coordinator (ideally, the local manager) to work through all the issues with the key interest groups in order to produce a plan that substantially improves the situation on the site. Management is often unglamorous and unfashionable. It seldom gets people academic recognition or promotions, because if it is done well, the outcomes seem so obviously right that it appears that anyone could have done the job. Yet making difficult things seem easy is the nature of true management genius.

While the management process described above applies to a single site, it can also be used in a broader context—regional or national—to plan the overall management of a group of important places. In fact, in the absence of such regional understanding and planning, it is often difficult to plan effectively for a particular site. For the managers, however, the crucial step is to begin where the resources and goodwill can be directed to protect a site. Even individual and simple plans can be powerful exemplars—for a district, or for an entire region.

Notes

1. In many places the management responsibility is split between agencies or individuals or indeed is so fragmented that it cannot really be said to exist. If this is the case, it is in itself a problem that must be addressed during the preparation of the plan.

2. Involvement of the local population can also change their outlook, educate them about aspects of significance, and make them more sympathetic to conservation.

3. This is often called a SWOT analysis—that is, an analysis of *s*trengths, *w*eaknesses, *o*pportunities, and *t*hreats.

References

Australia ICOMOS (International Council of Monuments and Sites)
1992   *The Illustrated Burra Charter.* Ed. Peter Marquis-Kyle and Meridith Walker. Sydney: Australia ICOMOS.

Pearson, M., and S. Sullivan
1995   *Looking after Heritage Places: The Basics of Heritage Planning for Managers, Landowners, and Administrators.* Melbourne: Melbourne University Press.

Management Considerations at a Mediterranean Site: Akrotiri, Thera

Christos Doumas

THE SITE OF AKROTIRI is located at the southern end of Thera, or Santorini, the southernmost island in the archipelago of the Cyclades, approximately sixty nautical miles north of Crete. Due to its strategic geographical position, Thera played an important role in the history of the Aegean. The activity of the now dormant volcano located on this island had a major influence on developments on the island and in the Aegean region in general. The archaeologist Spyridon Marinatos attributed the collapse of the Minoan civilization on Crete to one of the volcano's eruptions at the beginning of the late Bronze Age (around the mid–seventeenth century B.C.E.) (Marinatos 1939). This eruption, the magnitude of which is estimated to have been about four times that of Krakatoa, submerged a large part of Thera and buried the remaining areas under a thick mantle of volcanic ash. After a systematic survey of the island, Marinatos chose to excavate close to the modern village of Akrotiri, where he believed a large city was buried—perhaps the only one on the island during the Bronze Age.

Recording and Documentation

From 1967 until his death in 1974, Marinatos directed a major excavation at Akrotiri to verify his theory (Marinatos 1967–73). During this period, excavations were carried out at a frenetic pace, at the expense of documentation and conservation of the site and the finds. The photographic documentation, for which Marinatos was personally responsible, could be characterized as adequate. However, the complete lack of plans and drawings of the excavated sectors, as well as the lack of detailed daybooks, diminishes the value of the photographic archive, since it is extremely difficult to relate it to the rest of the excavation data.

Since 1975 a conscious effort has been made to ensure the fullest possible documentation, which appears annually in the *Proceedings of the Archaeological Society in Athens (Praktika tes en Athenais Archaiologikes Etaireias)*. All the information from the field is recorded on a cartographic grid with precise geographical coordinates. In parallel, all stages of the excavation process are described and drawn in detail. Recently an AutoCAD software system was introduced to assist in the timely and complete documentation of the excavation data. Finds are inventoried and photographed and some of them recorded graphically. The photographic archive includes all the documentation of the excavation procedure, architectural elements, stages of conservation and interventions, movable finds, and so forth. The graphic archive consists of maps, survey and topographic plans, excavation drawings and sketches, architectural drawings, drawings of the finds and plans, and drawings of the modern facilities on site. Separate inventories are kept for each category of finds, such as pottery, metal objects, lithic artifacts, bones, shells, floral remains, and so on.

For safety reasons there are two sets of these archives, one located on site and a second kept at the Archaeological Society at Athens. At present an electronic database is being designed to facilitate the handling and use of the information.

Significance of the Site

Akrotiri has values that make it an archaeological site of special cultural significance. The various areas of significance can be categorized as scientific, historical, aesthetic, social, and economic.

Scientific value

The site has scientific value since it can provide information on geological, climatological, environmental, and other phenomena. Nearly four thousand years ago, the inhabitants of Akrotiri faced many problems found in modern societies, which they resolved by means of seismic-protection measures, drainage plans, and architectural and engineering solutions. The study of the volume and nature of ejecta from the volcano, as well as of the manner of their deposition, has enabled scholars today to determine the mechanism and the magnitude of the eruption (Doumas 1978; Hardy 1990). The diversity of materials recovered from the excavation has contributed significantly to the improvement of methods and techniques of dating and the determination of provenance. The site has also contributed to the study of problems confronted by today's high-technological society. For example, the metal objects buried in the volcanic strata offer the possibility of studying the migration of trace elements in order to provide data useful to the quest for the safe burial of nuclear waste.

Historical value

Equally important—if not more important—is the historical value of Akrotiri. The site has been inhabited since Neolithic times (Doumas 1983; Sotirakopoulou 1996). From about the middle of the fifth millennium B.C.E., it developed gradually from a coastal village of fishermen and farmers to an urban settlement; before the middle of the second millennium B.C.E., it had become one of the most important harbor towns in the eastern Mediterranean. The site has provided new information concerning the development of town planning in the Aegean, the process of urbanization, and the ancient levels of technical and scientific knowledge, international relations, and culture in general. Information about architecture, ship-

Figure 1
Tripod table. This exquisite round tripod table is one of the rare examples of furniture from the houses of the sixteenth century B.C.E. at Akrotiri. It was recovered by pouring plaster of Paris into the hollow left in the volcanic ash by the decomposed wooden original. The process of decomposition caused displacement of the inlaid decoration of ivory rings, now mixed in the cast.

Figure 2, near right

Ostrich egg rhyton. For the prehistoric inhabitants of the Aegean, ostrich eggs were an exotic commodity, imported from eastern Mediterranean lands. Two eggs found in Room Delta 16 had been converted into rhytons (ritual libation vessels) by the application of faience attachments—a neck at the top and a rosette around the pouring hole at the bottom. These vessels were found together with hundreds of clay vases both imported and local, as well as imported marble and alabaster vessels, in a room that, judging from its street-level window, or counter, and the classification of its contents according to size, shape, material, provenance, and so on, could be considered a sixteenth-century-B.C.E. shop for such commodities.

Figure 3, far right

Canaanite jar. Canaanite jars are among the indisputable imports to Akrotiri from the eastern Mediterranean. One of the three sixteenth-century-B.C.E. examples found so far, it is decorated with a circle enclosing a cross, marked in the soft clay with the finger before firing. Curiously, this motif, a well-known sign of both Cretan scripts (Linear A and Linear B), was also used in the Old Canaanite alphabet to render the letter *teth*. Both vessel and sign reflect contacts between the Aegean and the eastern Mediterranean. In particular, the sign may be indicative of the common pool from which the letters of the early alphabet were drawn.

building, hydrodynamics, aerodynamics, astronomy, and mathematics is obtained, directly or indirectly, by study of the excavation data from the site (Doumas 1990). Designs of pieces of furniture that have been recovered by means of casts add to our information about the standard of living of the Bronze Age Aegean society (Fig. 1). The literacy of this society is attested by finds such as the clay tablets or the pots bearing inscriptions in Linear A script. Many imports from the eastern Mediterranean bear witness to the contacts of that world with the Aegean, connections that are also reflected in the works of art (Figs. 2, 3). Moreover, a recent entomological discovery offers a new view of early Aegean history. The cocoon of a wild silkworm found in a jar may be indicative of silk production and could explain the transparent appearance of some of the clothing worn by women depicted in the wall paintings (Fig. 4) (Panagiotakopoulou et al.,

Figure 4

Fresco fragment. Women are often depicted wearing delicate, diaphanous garments in Aegean wall paintings. The recent discovery of a wild-silkworm cocoon in a jar at Akrotiri suggests that silk might have been produced in Akrotiri in the sixteenth century B.C.E. and that diaphanous materials could have been made of silk and not of linen, as has been assumed.

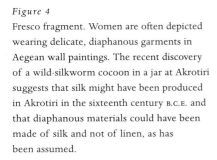

n.d.). These are a few of a long list of examples that give historical value to the site of Akrotiri.

Aesthetic value

In addition, excavations at Akrotiri have yielded unique examples of Aegean Bronze Age art of extraordinary aesthetic value. Works of early Cycladic marble carving and sculpture (Doumas 1983:27–28; Doumas 1992a:181–85, pls. 77–79), middle and late Cycladic pictorial pottery, and large-scale painting in the form of wall paintings that decorated private houses and public buildings bear witness to the artistic tastes of the site's inhabitants and support one of its most important values, the aesthetic or artistic (Figs. 5–8) (Doumas 1992b). These works also illustrate the technical achievements of the age, the flora and fauna, the everyday activities and occupations, as well as the spiritual concerns and human problems of the Bronze Age Aegean (Fig. 9) (Doumas 1987; Marinatos 1984).

Figure 5, above
Marble figurine. Marble figurines were fashioned in the Cyclades during the third millennium B.C.E. Their meaning for their creators may remain a mystery to us forever. Nevertheless, they represent the earliest artistic manifestation of the Aegean Bronze Age; their aesthetic quality is highly esteemed by modern art historians, as demonstrated by their distribution in collections and museums around the world. The fact that Akrotiri has so far produced almost all the characteristic types created during the entire millennium indicates the major role of Thera in the development of the early Cycladic civilization.

Figure 6, above
Marble vase. Early Cycladic sculpture was not restricted to figurines. Marble vases are another artistic manifestation of the third-millennium-B.C.E. Cycladic islanders. Artists were often inspired by the natural world around them, as this jar suggests: its body imitates the form of a sea urchin.

Figure 7, above
Figurative pot. Incised figures appeared as decoration in the Cyclades as early as the third millennium B.C.E. These painted decorations characterize the pottery of the middle and the early phases of the late Bronze Age (middle and late Cycladic)—i.e., the first half of the second millennium B.C.E. Migrating birds, heralds of the new season, and dolphins, constant companions of sailors, were among the favorite subjects. This is one of the special middle Cycladic class of vases called "swallow jugs," quite common at Akrotiri.

Figure 8, left
Figurative pot. Designed for the transport of perfumed oil and wine, this stirrup jar is an early invention of the late Cycladic period. While many had geometric or linear decoration, they were often covered with animal or floral motifs.

Figure 9

The Saffron Gatherers. This large wall painting shows one of the economic activities of the prehistoric Therans that was practiced by women. The scene depicted reveals a facet of Aegean daily life that would otherwise be unknown: education. The young girl on the right is trying to imitate the moves of her instructress/initiator on the left, who demonstrates them for her. One can clearly see the young novice's anxiety as she labors under the severe gaze of her supervisor—Is she doing it properly?

Social value

The values of the site mentioned above combine to create a further one for modern society, a value that can be characterized as social. Through the site and the wide range of finds, a part of the remote history of the Aegean can be better understood, giving the site great educational value for the public. Education allows what one author has called the "mastering of the cultural values of the past by each person rather than by only some individuals. By mastering these values and the creative time of past epochs that they represent, reutilizing it most efficiently and developing it further, man makes his contribution to the priceless treasure of eternity" (Baller 1984:8).

Economic value

The development of tourism, which can be considered part of the education process, gives Akrotiri an economic value for the islanders of Thera. The inhabitants of Akrotiri and the entire population of the island expect the site to be an inexhaustible source of economic development.

Condition of the Site

The burial of the entire city in ancient times under thick deposits of pumice and volcanic ash has preserved many buildings up to the second and sometimes even the third story (Fig. 10). However, the walls built with stones, clay occasionally mixed with broken straw, and timber have lost their original cohesiveness due to the disintegration of all organic matter

Figure 10
Walls with horizontal zones. The final phase at Akrotiri is represented by buildings that are of high quality, both architecturally and structurally. Horizontal zones of ashlar stones—stringcourses—slightly projecting from the wall, designated the level of each floor. Vertical poles and horizontal beams (now replaced by concrete) constituted a timber framework incorporated in the walls of every building. They bear witness to the antiseismic technology developed in Thera over the millennia.

(Figs. 11, 12). The state of preservation is not as good as it first appears, and the ruins are very vulnerable. Moreover, due to earthquakes or other factors, various structures (walls, doors, windows, staircases, and so on) are no longer in their original position.

Quite often, traces of organic materials like fauna and flora, pieces of furniture, baskets, leather, and so on, remain buried under the volcanic ash, and they require special conditions, staff, and techniques to be rescued and recorded.

Management Environment

The condition of the site and its significance present a number of constraints as well as opportunities that affect its management.

Figure 11
Negatives of two door frames that were impressed in the volcanic materials. Wooden structures (such as door and window frames and antiseismic timber frameworks) that are bearing elements need to be replaced before excavation can proceed, in order to protect the solid, heavy walls above.

Figure 12
Concrete replacement of a pier-and-door partition (polythyron). The excavators have created a support for the wall above the frame, as well as preserved the distorted form of the structure resulting from earthquake or general damage to the building.

The extent of the site presents a major challenge, since the currently exposed area represents but one-thirtieth of its estimated total surface. The protection of the totality of the archaeological area has created conflict between the site and the local inhabitants, who have been restrained from the full use of their properties.

The high degree of preservation of the architectural remains—as mentioned above, up to two or three stories in places—affects any plan for their conservation. Yet the physical condition of the ruins is very delicate, and their exposure to the elements would result in their total destruction. The protective roof that was built over the excavated area has become an obstacle to the full documentation of the site (no aerial photography is possible, for example) and disturbs the natural environment (Fig. 13). In addition, maintenance of the roof in the damaging environment of the

Figure 13
Protective cover over the site. The extensive roof over the whole excavated part of the site, though it protects the ruins, has drawbacks. Among them are high maintenance, the creation of less than optimal conditions for visitors and staff, and intrusion on the landscape.

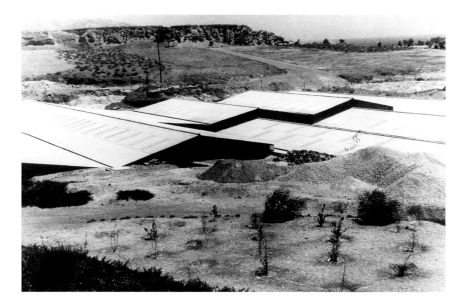

area (due to the acidity of the volcanic ash and to salt from the nearby sea) is a major concern. The canalization of the quantities of rainwater collected from the extensive roof is another related problem.

Following the great eruption of the volcano in ancient times, torrents of rainwater destroyed many of the buildings and created a ravine that divided the site in two. The management of the site must take into consideration the dynamics of this ravine.

The fragile condition of individual elements—such as walls, doors, windows, and staircases—presents a challenge for their maintenance. The creation of facilities needed for the conservation and storage of the wide variety and large quantities of finds inevitably disturbs the immediate environment of the site.

The thousands of visitors who come to the site daily during the summer months have a great impact and are a source of management concern (Fig. 14). Infrastructure work, such as the opening of roads, the creation of parking lots for the ever-increasing number of vehicles, and the construction of facilities for the growing number of visitors cause serious disturbances, not only to the immediate environment of the site but also to the entire island.

The crowding and circulation of visitors among the fragile ruins are potential dangers to both visitors and materials. The presentation of the site is constrained by the necessity to limit visitor access to the ruins and to the movable finds and by the limited space available on site for graphic and other kinds of information.

These constraints challenge the decision makers to find solutions that will address the problems, conserve the significance of the site, and create better methods and techniques of conservation and presentation— as well as enable the training of specialists, the education of the public, and the creation of jobs.

Figure 14
Tourist-season visitor traffic. Thousands of visitors walk daily through the ruins under the metal roof in the heavy tourist season (April through November). Temporary walkways created to prevent damage to the monuments hamper both circulation of visitors and the guiding of large groups.

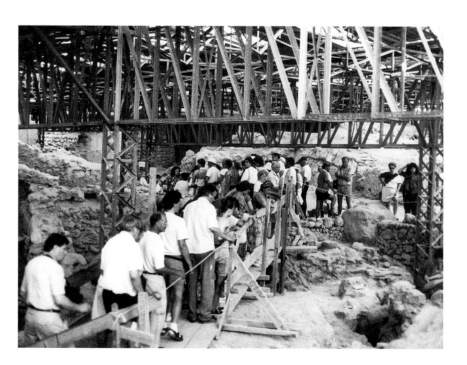

Management Policy

The importance of the site of Akrotiri, not only for the specialist but also for the general public, has made it a major tourist attraction. Various international scientific congresses and wide publicity in the mass media have made it almost a pilgrimage destination in the Aegean. However, as with many archaeological locations, the social value of the site seems to be perceived by many only in economic terms. The media, for example, have mainly been concerned with promoting Akrotiri as a tourist asset. The number of true educational programs made by the various television networks has been pitifully small.

Moreover, with the exception of some special organized groups, the great mass of tourists visit the site because the tour operators have included it in their schedules. This uncontrolled and unprogrammed exploitation of Akrotiri's economic value creates serious problems for the site (many related to the safety of visitors) as well as problems of conservation and protection of the monuments. The large number of visitors also creates problems of movement and deployment of the personnel currently involved in the ongoing archaeological investigation. The impossibility of providing sufficient information on site and of creating facilities nearby to do so prevents most visitors from being adequately informed about the cultural significance of the place they are visiting. It is clear, therefore, that these conflicts will not be resolved unless the process of managing the site is well planned and coordinated.

Nevertheless, the experience acquired over the last three decades has led to certain successful measures. The protection and maintenance of the site have been ensured by the designation of an extensive area as one of archaeological importance and by its partition into three zones, determined by proximity to the archaeological site itself. Zone I surrounds the expropriated archaeological excavation area and constitutes the first buffer for the archaeological site. Only traditional agricultural activity is permitted within this zone. Zone II encompasses an area where it is possible that there are antiquities, and the only buildings permitted are small structures for agricultural needs. In reality, a number of what are actually houses have been built near the beach under the guise of being farmers' sheds. The land included in the outermost zone, Zone III, has no restrictions on its use.

Other measures implemented over time have addressed specific problems. These have included the extensive expropriation of land around the excavation proper; the temporary diversion of the streambed a few meters west by the construction of a subterranean conduit at a higher level; the roofing of the excavated area; and the creation of various walkways for the circulation of visitors. Other conservation challenges have been met by the development of special excavation techniques and the creation of on-site storage facilities and laboratories for immediate conservation of finds.[1]

In order to accommodate circulation and to present the site to visitors, explanatory texts and graphics have been placed along the walkways; however, in order to prevent congestion, no more than three guided groups are allowed on site at any given time. At the end of each digging season, the excavators working on the site also organize seminars for the island's professional guides, so that they are aware of the new finds and of the progress of the research, and can better inform visitors, as well as assist in the conservation of the site.

Special programs for the education of the island's inhabitants have been organized by the excavation staff in collaboration with the Idryma Theras P. M. Nomikos Foundation. Seminars for the schoolteachers on the island have been received with great enthusiasm, and organized visits of school groups to the site, guided by archaeologists, have proved to be appreciated by schoolchildren of all levels.

Future Management Strategies

Experience obtained through the implementation of the measures discussed above has identified certain opportunities for the future management and conservation of the site. It has been determined that one of the most serious threats is the watercourse that ran through the archaeological site before excavation commenced, and its permanent diversion is a matter of priority. The westward extension of the excavation has exposed the modern subterranean conduit intended to divert the waters of the ravine, and this conduit now constitutes an immediate threat to the site—it could burst or overflow during heavy rains.

In the case of Akrotiri, the conflict between protection of the archaeological heritage and the economic interests of the local population is intense. The designation of the area as a protected archaeological zone has not met with the inhabitants' approval. On the one hand, it has prevented them from developing tourist enterprises near the archaeological site, while on the other, it has restricted land use for some families who have no other property. Moreover, the restrictions created by the protective designation have drastically reduced the demand for land in this area: land prices around the site are ridiculously low, particularly when compared with the astronomical sums paid elsewhere on the island. Thus, however much the local inhabitants appreciate the importance of the archaeological site, they inevitably see it as an obstacle to the touristic development of their community and to the upgrading of their economic status—goals that are being achieved on the rest of the island.

The managers of the archaeological site have a strong interest in improving relations with the people of Akrotiri. Talks with the municipal representatives and the people most affected have led to the agreement that more land should be expropriated around the site, since the state is the only potential buyer of the land in the archaeological zone. In addition, the authorities responsible for assessing properties for expropriation have agreed to increase the monetary evaluation of land in the archaeological zone, so that those deprived of their property will be able to replace it without serious loss.

A regional planning study is in progress, undertaken by the excavation staff in collaboration with the Greek Ministry of Environment and Public Works. This project envisages the creation of parking areas some distance from the archaeological site, as well as two-way approach roads that will eliminate the traffic jams of today. In parallel, the project foresees the definition of zones where activities related to tourism can be developed without alteration to the community's traditional nucleus, which fortunately has remained unspoiled.

The roof covering the site has suffered considerable damage over the three decades since its construction, and its replacement is urgently needed. A European Union research project under the general title of Archaeological Sites Protection Implementing Renewable Energy (ASPIRE) has been completed, and its pilot implementation has been successfully achieved (Figs. 15–17). The plans call for replacing the roof

Figure 15

Pilot application of new roofing plan: internal view of the pilot roof. A pilot application of the new protective covering has demonstrated not only that conditions will improve for people working or walking under the new roof, but also that its appearance both inside and outside will be aesthetically superior, unifying the broken aspect of the natural landscape.

Figure 16

Pilot application of new roofing plan: external view of the pilot roof (see Fig. 15).

Figure 17
Pilot application of new roofing plan. The
unobtrusive design blends into the surrounding environment (see Figs. 15, 16).

with another that will be adapted to the natural environment and that will
use ecologically sensitive forms of energy and materials—sun, water,
wind, and earth. The new roof will protect monuments and visitors from
the sun and carbon dioxide, while providing localized air-conditioned areas
for visitors and excavators. The construction of the new roof has been
included among the projects of the Greek Ministry of Culture to be
financed by European Union programs.

The project to replace the roof has prompted the study of a series
of measures that can be taken to minimize the conflict among the site's
various values. Under the new roof, a network of main and secondary
walkways will facilitate the circulation of a large number of visitors. These
new circulation modes and patterns will reduce the dangers to both visitors and ruins. Located a few meters above the ruins and alternating with
overpasses, the walkways will offer better perspectives over the site, and
visitors will be able see the interiors of buildings and view the layout of
the ancient settlement.

Thematic exhibitions of finds from the site will be arranged at
intervals along the perimeter walkway, so that the visit to the site becomes
more than a brief episode during a tourist's summer vacation. It is hoped
that these presentations will provide a substantial introduction to the
world of the Aegean Bronze Age.[2]

The roofed area will be converted into a "living" museum, which,
with modern communication technology, will be used to educate the visitor in an entertaining way. Ongoing evaluation is planned through ques-
tionnaires for visitors, guides, tour operators, travel agents, members of
the local community, and scholars. The information thus gathered will
help in the continued improvement of visiting conditions.

If the above goals are realized, the archaeological site at Akrotiri
will become a place of education and recreation. However, the achievement of these two objectives requires the governmental bodies responsible
for education and tourism to participate in the cost of operation and main-

tenance of the site. With secure financial support, the excavation, scientific research, and conservation can proceed at a steady pace. The development of individual research projects to process the finds should provide answers to the still-open questions of historical scholarship and conservation. At the same time, the site could develop into a school for young scholars and a training ground for excavation and conservation techniques. And finally, opportunities for new jobs will emerge from the various activities that will arise from the effective management of the site.

Notes

1. Three such laboratories now exist at Akrotiri—one for mending and conserving pottery, one for metallic objects and other materials, and one for wall paintings.

2. Some of the themes suggested for these exhibitions are the island's geological history; its environment (climate, fauna, flora); the everyday occupations and activities of the inhabitants of prehistoric Thera; the inhabitants' diet and dress, technical and protoscientific achievements, ideology and beliefs; and their relations with the rest of the world (see also Doumas 1993).

References

Baller, E.

1984   *Communism and Cultural Heritage.* Moscow: Progress Publishers.

Doumas, Christos

1983   *Thera: Pompeii of the Ancient Aegean.* London: Thames and Hudson.

1987   Η Ξεστή 3 και οι κυανοκέφαλοι στην τέχνη της Θήρας (E Xeste 3 kai oi kyanokephaloi sten techne tes Theras; Xeste 3 and the blue-headed people in the art of Thera). In *Ειλαπίνη, τόμος τιμητικός για τον Καθηγητή Νικόλαο Πλάτωνα* (Eilapine, tomos timetikos gia ton Kathegete Nikolao Platona; Eilapine, volume in honor of Professor Nicholas Platon), 151–59. Heraklion: Demos Herakleiou.

1990   The elements at Akrotiri. In *Thera and the Aegean World III: Proceedings of the Third International Congress, Santorini, Greece, 3–9 September 1989,* ed. D. Hardy, vol. 1, 24–30. London: Thera Foundation.

1992a   Ανασκαφή Ακρωτηρίου Θήρας (Anaskaphe Akroteriou Theras; Excavation at Akrotiri, Thera). *Πρακτικά της εν Αθήναις Αρχαιολογικής Εταιρείας* (Praktika tes en Athenais Archaiologikes Etaireias; Proceedings of the Archaeological Society in Athens).

1992b   *The Wall-Paintings of Thera.* Trans. Alex Doumas. Athens: Thera Foundation.

1993   Archaeological sites as alternative exhibitions: The case of Akrotiri, Thera. *European Review* 1(3):279–84.

Doumas, Christos, ed.

1978   *Thera and the Aegean World: Papers Presented at the Second International Scientific Congress, Santorini, Greece, August 1978.* Vol. 1, pt. 1 (geosciences), 21–361. London: Thera and the Aegean World, 1978–80.

Hardy, D., ed.

1990   *Thera and the Aegean World III: Proceedings of the Third International Congress, Santorini, Greece, 3–9 September 1989.* Vol. 1. London: Thera Foundation.

Marinatos, Nanno

1984   *Art and Religion in Thera.* Athens: D. and I. Mathioulakis.

Marinatos, Spyridon

1939   The volcanic destruction of Minoan Crete. *Antiquity* 13:425–39.

1967–73   *Excavations at Thera*. Athens: Archaeological Society at Athens.

Panagiotakopoulou, E., P. C. Buckland, P. M. Day, C. Doumas, A. Sarpaki, and P. Skidmore

n.d.   Silk and cotton in the Aegean Bronze Age: A new find from Thera and a reevaluation of evidence. *Antiquity*. Forthcoming.

Sotirakopoulou, P.

1996   Late Neolithic pottery from Akrotiri on Thera: Its relations and the consequent implications. In *Die Ägäische Frühzeit*, ed. E. Alram Stern, 581–607. Vienna: Österreichischen Akademie der Wissenschaften.

Reconstruction of Ancient Buildings

Hartwig Schmidt

O NE OF THE MOST famous German visitors to Italy in the eighteenth century was Johann Wolfgang von Goethe (1749–1832).
He arrived in Rome in November 1786; a few days later he noted
in his diary: "Let's admit, however, it is a sour and sad business to pick the
old Rome out of the new one, but one has to do it nevertheless, and can
hope for invaluable satisfaction. One meets traces of a magnificence and of
a destruction, both of which are beyond us" (Goethe 1976:117).[1] His words
anticipate a problem that today's visitors of ancient sites still face—ruins
can be difficult to understand without the benefit of interpretation.

Many travelers—fascinated by ancient ruins—visited eighteenth-
century Rome on the grand tour. Guides, called ciceroni, led visitors
through the sights. The mix of fact and fiction in their explanations varied
from guide to guide. Around the middle of the century, archaeologists,
who had become interested in the ruins of Rome, began excavating and
restoring them, attempting historic reconstruction of original buildings.
This endeavor, which could be achieved theoretically on the drawing
board, failed in reality because there were seldom enough remaining traces
and clues.

During excavations that were started in 1800 in the Roman
Forum, architects of the French Academy in Rome proposed the reconstruction of the Arch of Titus (Fig. 1), only the center of which was in
fairly sound condition. First, in 1809–10, Auguste-Jean-Maria Guénepin
produced an exact record of the building. Then, in 1812, the dismantling
of the arch was begun. In 1817 the architect Raffaele Stern (1774–1820)
initiated a project of research and excavation that was finally completed
twelve years later by Giuseppe Valadier (1762–1839). These architects
incorporated the original remains into a complete reconstruction of the
ancient building; in fact, even today, the arch appears from a distance to
have survived fairly intact. A closer examination, however, reveals
differences between the original, damaged portion in the center and the
newer parts in the outer areas.

To identify the new parts visually, the architects used a method
that can be considered exemplary even today. While the new building

Figure 1

Giovanni Battista Piranesi, *View of the Arch of Titus*, ca. 1770. Etching, 47 × 71 cm. Resource Collections, Getty Research Institute for the History of Art and the Humanities, Los Angeles. This image of the ruined Arch of Titus gives an idea of how difficult it must have been to imagine, from the state of the ancient ruins, their former, intact appearance. On the left is the entrance to the Farnese Gardens, in the background the ruins of the Roman Forum. The remains of the triumphal arch had already been freed from their medieval superstructure and buttressed by masonry on the left.

elements were, of course, created to the original scale, they were rendered as simplified shapes and produced in a material different from the original. Despite the patination of the new parts since the reconstruction, it is still possible to distinguish between original and supplemental elements (Fig. 2a, b). Of course, it is much easier for a visitor to comprehend a complete structure than a building in a ruined state. Archaeologists, however, are only interested in the original parts.

The condition of the Roman Forum today illustrates another problem inherent in all reconstruction: Archaeological ruins once corresponded to and harmonized with their original surroundings. When reconstructed, however, these complete new structures are often difficult to integrate into the existing setting. This problem is very evident in the case of the Stoa of Attalos on the Athenian Agora, rebuilt by the American School of Classical Studies in Athens between 1953 and 1956. The large size of the newly erected, complete hall presents a jarring contrast to the low ruins of the ancient structures that surround it (Fig. 3).

The Stoa of Attalos, a present of Attalos II (r. 159–138 B.C.E.), king of Pergamon, to the city of Athens, was erected in the second century B.C.E. Only small fragments of the building have survived the ravages of time (Fig. 4). The skillful reconstruction carried out by the American School used building materials available in ancient times. Since the new building had to accommodate storerooms, a museum, and workrooms for

a   b

Figure 2a, b
Arch of Titus, Rome. From a distance (a) the
arch looks today as if it has survived intact
through time. A closer view (b) reveals, however, considerable damage in the central parts,
which can be clearly differentiated from the
newer, reconstructed parts in the outer areas.
The new elements were constructed in
simplified shapes, as seen in the Corinthian
capitals and in the unfluted column in the
right corner. The new elements were also rendered in different materials—for example,
travertine has been substituted for the original
marble. While it is still possible today to distinguish between the original parts and the
reconstructions, to the uncritical observer the
arch appears intact.

archaeologists, modern installations of water, gas, and electricity were
provided. For safety, the restorers used concrete in the ceilings rather than
reproducing the original wooden-beam construction. The rooms of
ancient shops on the building's ground level were adapted to house a
museum. Given the general condition of the building as well as the modern installations, visitors should understand that the structure is not, in
fact, authentically ancient. Even so, tour guides report that it is often
difficult to rid tourists of their romantic notion that Socrates once rallied
his students around him on the very steps on which the modern visitors
are standing (Fig. 5).

Historic buildings are invaluable sources for historic research. Not
only do they embody data but they are also authentic, tangible remains of
the past that have survived through history. This history is manifested in
the signs of aging and the injuries left by use, alteration, and destruction—
evidence that documents the passage of time. Some of the damage can be
repaired, and lost parts can be replaced. The result, however, is not a more
complete ancient building but, instead, a modern creation.

Toward the end of the nineteenth century, archaeologists began
to formulate rules to ensure the authenticity of ruins and prevent their
falsification. Nicolaos Balanos (1860–1942), who led the re-erection of the
Acropolis in Athens from 1895 to 1940, described his working method,
which he called *anastylosis,* as the reassembly of existing but dismembered
parts (Balanos 1938). He contrasted his method with *reconstruction*—the
re-creation, with new materials, of parts that no longer exist. His concept

Figure 3

The reconstructed Stoa of Attalos in the Athenian Agora. The Stoa of Attalos, originally built around 150 B.C.E., was reconstructed between 1953 and 1956. The building appears enormous in relation to the surrounding small dwellings and sparse remains of other ancient buildings. The structure has modern water, gas, and electrical installations so it can serve its current function as office, storage, and museum space for the American School of Classical Studies in Athens.

Figure 4

Ancient foundations of the Stoa of Attalos prior to reconstruction. In 1952, when the site was excavated, the foundations of the ancient structure were preserved over the whole length of the building, and the walls stood at their full height in two places.

Figure 5

Front of the reconstructed Stoa of Attalos. The stairs of the *crepidoma* are used as a resting place by modern visitors. Although the imposing building is obviously a modern reconstruction, tour guides report that tourists commonly hold the anachronistic notion that the stoa is authentically ancient.

of anastylosis was established in 1931 in the *Recommendations of the Athens Conference;* later it was also embodied in *The Venice Charter,* which laid down binding principles for the conservation and restoration of monuments (ICOMOS 1964, 1965; see Appendix A). *The Venice Charter* states that "ruins must be maintained and measures necessary for the permanent conservation and protection of architectural features and of objects discovered must be taken. Furthermore, every means must be taken to facilitate the understanding of the monument and to reveal it without ever distorting its meaning. All reconstruction work should, however, be ruled out a priori. Only anastylosis, that is to say, the reassembling of existing but dismembered parts, can be permitted. The material used for integration should always be recognizable and its use should be the least that will ensure the conservation of a monument and the reinstatement of its form" (ICOMOS 1964, 1965:art. 15).

The simplest form of anastylosis is the re-erection of columns. Yet even this most benign of all reconstruction procedures can fundamentally alter a structure's appearance. Between 1922 and 1930, when Balanos re-erected the fallen columns on the northern side of the Parthenon, he completely changed the appearance of the building and, at the same time, nearly erased the evidence of the 1687 explosion that tore a gaping hole in the colonnade (Figs. 6, 7).

Figure 6
Nineteenth-century view of the Parthenon, Athens, showing extensive damage to the colonnade. This 1890 photograph taken from the northwest records the broad gap created when columns collapsed from an explosion in 1687.

Figure 7
The Parthenon after the repairs of 1922–30. This photograph shows the Parthenon as it appeared following the anastylosis carried out by Nicolaos Balanos. Columns were re-erected and the architraves and frieze replaced. Missing parts were produced in masonry and plastered with a cement mortar. It remained in this condition until recent years, when new conservation work was undertaken.

There is a serious danger that, through ignorance or the application of unsound methods of restoration and anastylosis, restorers can distort ruins and destroy their integrity as documents. Such erroneous interventions result in a loss of value. To safeguard against these risks, *The Venice Charter* rejects reconstruction on excavation sites, considering anastylosis as the only permissible type of intervention.

A re-erection, when done strictly as anastylosis, differs visually from a reconstruction that introduces new materials. The Library of Celsus in Ephesus is a good example of anastylosis. While Friedmund Hueber, who re-erected the structure from 1970 to 1978, adhered to the principles of *The Venice Charter,* he found it necessary to stabilize the building with reinforced concrete and some new columns. The building does not look like a historical forgery; nevertheless, it is, in fact, a recently created, modern "ruin" (Figs. 8–11).

Visitors close to the monument can easily detect that it is only a partial re-erection, consisting mainly of the magnificent facade of columns. There has been no attempt to reconstruct the whole building, as in the case of the Stoa of Attalos. The work was limited to assembling the marble elements when their original positions could be determined. The rough stone masonry at the back was not reconstructed, and the building remains in a partially ruined condition (Fig. 12).

Figure 8
The Library of Celsus in Ephesus during the excavations in 1905. Architects put together the remaining architectural elements to get an idea of the appearance of the original Roman building. Some of these elements are today in museums in Vienna and Istanbul; they are either missing in the modern reconstruction or replaced by copies.

Figure 9
The Library of Celsus seen at the end of the Street of the Curetes. The magnificent marble facade was restored between 1970 and 1978 by Friedmund Hueber and V. M. Strocka, who incorporated original stones found on the site, copies of architectural members that had been removed into museum collections, and new pieces needed for structural stability. The seventeen-meter-high facade dominates the surrounding ruins and attracts the attention of tourists.

Figure 10, above
The Library of Celsus and its immediate surrounds. Even after the 1980–89 reconstruction
of the Gate of Mazäus and Mithridates (on
the right) and the Tetragonos Agora (not
visible), the library dominates the site.

Figure 11, above right
The Library of Celsus viewed from below. A
close look reveals the use of original, broken
elements as well as the treatment of new
areas. The impression created is that of a
ruined building.

Even so, the re-erection of the seventeen-meter-high facade
changed the character of the entire archaeological site, and the Library
of Celsus has become the most prominent ruin of Ephesus: it towers over
the remains of all other structures, and since they are lower, their apparent
importance is diminished. Although the intent and methods of reconstruction differ from those of the Stoa of Attalos, the reconstruction has created the same problem—a misleadingly dominant structural presence.

In this light, it is logical to ask if there are valid reasons for
reconstruction and whether reconstructed ruins can have a viable existence. There are good reasons to reconstruct structures, but none of
them are justified within a true archaeological site. In contrast, in an
approach known as "experimental archaeology," reconstruction is occasionally employed to test archaeological theories. The Lejre Historical-
Archaeological Research Center, founded in 1964 by Hans-Ole Hansen in
Lejre, near Roskilde, Denmark, is a well-known interpretation of this idea
(Hansen 1982). In Lejre various excavations yielded data about materials
and their use; this information was used as a basis for the reconstruction
of three prehistoric villages (Fig. 13).

Another example of experimental archaeology, carried out in
the 1930s, is the reconstruction of a Bronze Age settlement in
Unteruhldingen, on Lake Constance in Germany (Fig. 14) (Reinerth
1980:12). The full-scale models are based on the interpretation of data
from excavations at various sites. Although many of the archaeological

Figure 12
The Library of Celsus viewed from the
side. The reconstruction focused mainly on
the facade; the rest of the structure remains
in ruins.

Figure 13

Lejre Historical-Archaeological Research
Center, near Roskilde, Denmark. This aerial
view shows the site where three prehistoric
villages have been re-created based on information about materials and their uses that has
been gathered from various excavations.

Figure 14

Reconstruction of a Bronze Age settlement at
Unteruhldingen, Lake Constance, Germany.
Information gathered from excavations in
Buchau at the Federsee, fifty kilometers away,
was used by Hans Reinerth in 1931 to create
this full-scale model, which, it is now known,
is not historically accurate.

hypotheses that guided the reconstruction have since proved incorrect, the
settlement is still a major tourist attraction. It appears that visitors can be
interested in fanciful and attractive exhibitions, even when they know that
such exhibitions are neither authentic nor scientifically accurate.

How people have lived in the past is a matter of great interest to
the public. Some methods of presenting archaeological sites can convey
ancient ways of life more comprehensively than architectural reconstruction. Such an example is an installation at a shopping center that was built
from 1976 to 1981 in York, England, above the excavation of a Viking
settlement dating from the tenth century (Fig. 15). At the basement level,
visitors can view a re-creation of life in the time of the Vikings, composed
of the settlement's remains supplemented with furnishings and fittings.
The substantial flow of visitors through the Jorvik Viking Centre—900,000
a year—bears witness to the fascination that this sort of presentation can
engender. Visitors take a thirteen-minute ride through the exhibition in
small cars, learning how the former inhabitants and their surroundings
looked "on a day late in October in the year 948 in the Viking-time [of]
old Yorvik," as the brochure declares (Jorvik Viking Centre 1992). The
individual figures, which are immobile wooden carvings, inhabit surroundings that have been re-created in the greatest possible detail—even including noises and odors. In addition to the historical exhibit, a reconstructed
excavation site re-creates for visitors the archaeological work that took
place here. This component is intended to convey to visitors the fact that
all the reconstructions are fictitious, and that they reflect interpretations
based on very vague information. However, it is unclear if this clarification
is effective.

Figure 15
Jorvik Viking Centre, York, England. A shopping center was built in 1976–81 above the excavation of a tenth-century Viking settlement. Two of the rows of buildings were reconstructed to correspond to archaeologists' conjecture about how they were originally built. The "Vikings" are wooden models.

The type of comprehensive presentation seen at the Jorvik Viking Centre was first developed in the United States. Such installations are often called historic site museums or open-air museums on historical sites. Prime examples are Yorktown and Colonial Williamsburg in Virginia, where colonial North America is re-created. Another such site is Plimoth Plantation, an outdoor museum complex that attempts to recreate the Pilgrims' first settlement as it stood in 1627, seven years after their arrival in North America (Fig. 16) (Plimoth Plantation 1994). The individual houses and their furnishings are not authentic, nor is the location, since the museum is situated in modern-day Plymouth, some distance from the original settlement. The employees of the site—called "interpreters"— dress in historically accurate costumes, performing normal chores while they explain their work, in order to make life in the past as accessible as

Figure 16
Plimoth Plantation, Plymouth, Massachusetts. The museum complex attempts to re-create the Pilgrims' first settlement at Plymouth Rock, where they landed in 1620. Individual houses and their furnishings have been re-created five kilometers from the original landing site. Employees—called "interpreters"—dress in historical costumes and perform everyday chores while explaining their work to visitors.

possible to visitors. The absence of authentic objects led to the development of this form of presentation, which has as its main focus the telling of a story rather than the exhibition of historical materials.

Jorvik Viking Centre and Plimoth Plantation are fictional worlds created for visitors. These parks with historical themes meet a certain demand in a society with leisure time and income available for visual entertainment. In the modern world, heritage professionals should accept that nontraditional methods of historical education are valid. The ideals of authenticity and originality are not an issue in such places—entertainment is. The values of experimental archaeology, however, are not transferable to authentic archaeological sites.

Reconstruction, then, falls in the realm of tourist attractions, and as such should not be part of archaeological sites. Activities on authentic sites should be restricted to measures that preserve historic buildings and monuments: conservation, restoration, and anastylosis. Only these practices can ensure the unaltered preservation of the historical remains, thereby safeguarding their integrity as authentic records of history. In addition to yielding important scientific data, archaeological sites bear witness to the transitory nature of all human creations. The handling of ruins, therefore, should respect their nature. Their presentation should be responsible and modest and incorporate signs of aging. Archaeological practices should try to achieve a long-lasting conservation. They should not aim for sensational presentations as a means of attracting visitors.

Note

1. "Gestehen wir es jedoch, es ist ein saures und trauriges Geschäft, das alte Rom aus dem neuen herauszuklauben, aber man muß es denn doch tun und zuletzt eine unschätzbare Befriedigung hoffen. Man trifft Spuren einer Herrlichkeit und einer Zerstörung, die beide über unsere Begriffe gehen" (Goethe 1976:117).

References

Balanos, Nicolaos
1938   *Les monuments de l'Acropole: Relèvement et conservation.* Paris: C. Massin.

Goethe, Johann Wolfgang von
1976   *Italienische Reise.* Ed. Jochen Golz. Berlin: Rütten and Loening.

Hansen, Hans-Ole
1982   *Lejre Research Center.* Lejre, Denmark: Lejre Historical-Archaeological Research Center.

ICOMOS (International Council of Monuments and Sites)
1964,   *International Charter for the Conservation and Restoration of Monuments and Sites.*
1965   Venice: ICOMOS.

Jorvik Viking Centre
1992   *Guidebook.* York, England: Jorvik Viking Centre.

Plimoth Plantation
1994   *A Pictorial Guide.* Plymouth, Mass.: Plimoth Plantation.

Reinerth, Hans
1980   *Pfahlbauten am Bodensee.* 12th ed. Überlingen: August Fexel.

The Presentation of Archaeological Sites

Renée Sivan

EVERY YEAR, public interest in the archaeological heritage along with the ease of modern travel are bringing visitors to heritage sites by the millions. In some places, in fact, the desire to attract tourism has become one of the major driving forces behind the development of such sites. At the same time, national and international authorities, as well as concerned heritage professionals, are becoming increasingly aware of the need to find new measures to preserve archaeological remains. This necessity, as well as the need to make visitors' experiences richer and more meaningful, has focused attention on the ways in which historical sites are interpreted and presented to the visiting public.

Monumental archaeological sites, common in the Mediterranean region, are often particularly impressive, attractive, and memorable. For decades, reconstruction of ruins was thought to be a good method for protecting physical remains and making sites understandable to visitors. Unfortunately, all too often, expensive reconstruction was mainly the expression of the planners' creativity and bore little connection to a site's original form. While some of these reconstructions were no doubt intriguing, they did not always result in clear or accurate interpretations of the historical evidence; today, many of them compromise the historical and aesthetic integrity of the sites and raise important questions about information that is being transmitted to visitors.

Despite the significance of some sites and despite the fascinating histories associated with them, visitors can find their appearance disappointing. Heritage professionals recognize that archaeological sites hold historic data whose integrity must be respected and that neglecting their conservation leaves them unprotected and subject to deterioration, decay, and vandalism. In addition to providing important benefits to visitors, the presentation and interpretation of sites are becoming accepted means of conservation as well.

The presentation of a site should aim to bring history to life by use of the remaining archaeological evidence. And, at the same time that it portrays the reality of the past, the presentation should allow visitors to grasp the effect of the passage of time by creating direct visual contact with the site. In other words, the presentation should enable visitors to become involved with, and to communicate with, the ruins and to gain a sense of their meaning.

In his *Travels in Hyperreality,* Umberto Eco has pointed out that, while fakes lack historical authenticity, they can possess "visual reality," and that many people, regardless of "historical reality," believe that what they can see is real. Some presentations, particularly those relying on reconstruction, falsify archaeological reality. A reconstructed ruin does not bring back the original structure; rather, it is a new, different—but very "real"—modern creation. Without doubt, the more complete an architectural structure, the more power and comprehensibility it has for the viewer. But visitor impact and understanding are not the only considerations in the presentation of a site, and these goals cannot be allowed to override completely other factors. Heritage professionals have the additional obligation to protect the scientific value of the archaeological record. The presentation of a site, therefore, should make it attractive, visually stimulating, and thought provoking while maintaining historical accuracy and respecting the integrity of the ruins.

Principles of Site Presentation

Every site is unique, both in its present and past realities. The appropriate interpretation depends on the physical evidence that has survived. A successful presentation that is accurate, sensitive, and attractive takes into consideration the size of the site, its physical importance, and its aesthetic value. A professional, after evaluating these elements, must make decisions about the message that should be conveyed, the story that should be told, and the methods that will best allow this to be achieved.

The optimal method of making a site hospitable and attractive is to begin by considering it in its entirety. Its presentation can be enhanced through the extensive use of the physical remains and the landscape that surrounds them to communicate the site's human history. After all, sites are the remains of societies that were real and alive; they are not simply strata and ruined monuments—and in any case, most visitors are more interested in human stories than in architectural history. The ruins are reflections of political struggles, cultural fashions, technological skills, artistic expressions, religious beliefs, and other aspects of human behavior. The challenge of interpretation is to bring all this forth; to focus exclusively on architectural elements would be to shortchange visitors by telling them an incomplete story.

It is important to recognize that there is no such thing as an objective presentation: All presentations are based on interpretive choices, and these choices combine to tell a story. It is up to the presentation professional, in consultation with other specialists, to select which particular story will be told.

Indeed, most sites have more than one story to tell. In most cases, the remains of a site favor the telling of one particular story, although some important historical events have left no physical traces. In certain instances, it might be possible to tell parallel stories, but care must be taken not to confuse or overwhelm the visitor. Most visitors arrive at a site with limited knowledge of its history, and they spend a relatively short period of time there.

The amount of information that the presentation conveys will often depend on the size of the site and the relationship between the physical remains and the history being told. A large site generally has spaces that provide for an intermezzo in the tour, places where the visitor can reflect and absorb the information provided. One such site is Beth Shearim, an important Jewish necropolis from the third or fourth century C.E. The large cemetery is composed of dozens of catacombs containing carved or engraved Jewish symbols and Hebrew, Aramaic, and Greek inscriptions, as well as hundreds of sarcophagi with pagan depictions. In order to maintain the quiet atmosphere of a cemetery, no interpretation is located inside the catacombs. Instead, in other places on the site, subjects (such as the meaning of Jewish symbols) and themes (such as pluralism and tolerance as reflected in a place where Jewish and pagan motifs are found side by side) are developed for visitors. The interpretive plaza is the first of a series of breaks provided for visitors; the presentation contains metallic photographic presentations, models, and aluminum panels as visitor guides (Fig. 1).

Presentations should keep intervention on the site to a minimum, keeping the remains as the principal "actors" rather than using them simply as stage design. Some presentation techniques currently in fashion can overwhelm the archaeological remains. One such technique, called "reversible reconstruction," is intended to create an illusion of volume or to hint at the original dimension of a structure with modern materials such as textiles or metal. These creations can produce a stronger visual impact than the original vestiges, and the visitor, who cannot help but focus on the new structures, often overlooks the real site.

In contrast to this method, appropriate presentations allow the remains to hold the focus of attention. Sometimes the re-erection of one column in situ will suffice to communicate the scale of a temple. In other instances, a properly positioned statue (or even a replica) can help visitors imagine the entire environment.

Figure 1
Interpretive plaza at Beth Shearim, Israel, an important Jewish necropolis from the third or fourth century C.E. The interpretive plaza is the first of a series of intermezzos provided for visitors. There are metallic photographic presentations, models, and aluminum panels to inform visitors.

An intelligent treatment of the surroundings can also contribute to the understanding of ruins. Many sites in the Mediterranean originally contained substantial architectural structures of durable materials, such as stone, and the elements that have survived the passage of time are found scattered about. Sometimes simply creating clearings around key elements that have remained in situ can assist visitors to visualize the original contours and spaces of buildings. These visual definitions can be intensified by differentiating interior from exterior spaces or by delineating rooms within a structure, through the use in certain areas of materials different from those found on the site, such as gravel. A site does not have to be transformed for the desired message to be effectively conveyed.

Methods of Site Presentation

The individual or group responsible for presentation will spend time studying it and will eventually possess a deep understanding of the site as a whole. In contrast, most visitors arrive with little knowledge and understanding of the site. Along with choosing the story to be told and the amount of information to be transmitted, presentation professionals should select methods and techniques that will convey a broad vision of the archaeological space and its history.

Once the story has been selected, the site presenter must choose the place and the means to tell it. Various locations on or near the site can become the theater for the story. Likewise, there are many choices (and more are becoming available daily through new technologies) for the method or medium of presentation. The selection of location and methods will depend on the site. Some sites with abundant remains do not lend themselves easily to in situ interpretation, because signage or other apparatus could interfere with the ruins. One such site is Beth Shean, a biblical, Roman-Byzantine site located in the Jordan valley (Fig. 2).

A visitors center, a place close to the site where information can be made available, can be extremely helpful. Many techniques—animated films and holograms or other three-dimensional interpretations—allow large amounts of information to be communicated in clear and attractive ways.

Figure 2
Ruins at Beth Shean, Israel. The interpretive model and signage, which are placed adjacent to the ruins, do not intrude upon the visitors' view of the ruins themselves. When such presentations are located in such a way that they are in direct dialogue with a site, they can be very effective.

A stop at such a center, however, should not substitute for the visit to the site. Instead, presentations at the center should prepare the visitor and provide sufficient information to make the contact with the actual site more enjoyable. It is of little use to display models of houses, theaters, or any other structures in the center unless the visitor at the same time has a direct view of the site. If this arrangement is not possible, the time elapsed between the viewing of such models at the center and a later confrontation with the original remains (which can often be disappointingly meager) makes it difficult for the untrained visitor to put the information to good use. In addition to being an opportunity to provide background information, visitors centers can be seen as places where the site visit can be planned. They should provide information about guided tours, routes for independent touring, and other practical matters.

Once inside the archaeological area, visitors should be encouraged to concentrate on the site itself. Certain sites, due to their size or nature, can be easily interpreted with the help of pamphlets or audioguides. Clear and well-edited pamphlets, with little text and many supporting images, can act as effective mediators between visitors and the site. Information can also be conveyed very effectively by means of well-designed interpretive panels in situ, as long as they are unobtrusive, concise, and attractive—and not steeped in academic rhetoric.

Some presentation techniques can be used to suggest an environment through either visual elements or sound, and they can be employed in areas of sites where there are few or no remains. These techniques can stir the imaginations of visitors and generate a stream of associations: thus they can arouse curiosity as well as enhance understanding. For example, near the ruin of a church, synagogue, or mosque there might be the sound of prayer; near an ancient fountain, that of running water.

In the past, three-dimensional presentations consisted mainly of models of sites or edifices. Recent technological developments, however, have enlarged the choice of methods to help visitors visualize the life of an ancient site. These elements can convey detailed, even scholarly, information, and they can do so without diminishing the authenticity of the site, since they do not impinge upon the remains.

Effective methods include models, dioramas, and multimedia presentations that evoke the atmosphere of the past, located in such a way that they are in direct dialogue with the site. When these elements are located close to a site instead of being isolated in a distant structure, visitors are able to relate the information to what they are actually seeing, and that information can assist them in visualizing the site at another time. These techniques have the additional advantage of not requiring much written text, so that visitors are free to concentrate on what is visible around them.

Such methods of visual presentation that evoke the ancient life of a place can be seen at Avdat, an ancient site in the Negev Desert of Israel, which has a long history of use. In order to re-create daily life during various periods, Avdat is presented through a variety of methods, including replicas, environmental sculptures, models, graphic panels, and interpretive environments (Figs. 3–8). Since various stories are told in this large and difficult site, with a long circuit and extreme temperatures, the use of a variety of presentation methods maintains visitor interest.

Figure 3, right
Environmental sculptures, Avdat, Israel.
Avdat was founded by the Nabateans in the
fourth century B.C.E. as a way station on the
Spice Route from Arabia to the Mediterranean
port of Gaza. During the Byzantine period,
Avdat flourished; the city was fortified, and
churches were erected on the acropolis. The
inhabitants' main income was derived from
agriculture, primarily wine production. The
sculptural installation depicts a caravan
arriving at the city.

a

b

Figure 4a, b
Wine press at Avdat. The environmental presentation, made of treated metal, at the left in the
overview (a), and the interpretive panels (b), made
of artificial stone, require no maintenance.

a   b

Figure 5a, b
Church of Saint Theodore, Avdat. The interpretive model of the original structure of the
church is located in situ so that the visitor can
find references between it and the remains of
the original structure (a). The model (b) is
made of bronze, to discourage theft and vandalism and to minimize maintenance.

Figure 6
Wine cellar cave, Avdat. Cement replicas simulating pottery are used in places where ancient jars were found during excavation.

Figure 7
Environmental presentation at the wine merchant's house, Avdat. In some instances, there was insufficient material evidence to tell a given story. Only literary sources, and sometimes anachronistic ones, were available for the early period of the Nabateans. An artist was commissioned to create interpretive, humoristic sculptures.

Figure 8
Environmental presentation at Avdat, depicting a goatherd and his charges.

Dioramas or multimedia presentations can also provide answers to the many questions that puzzle visitors to archaeological sites. Not all visitors are interested in physical features, methods of construction, or architectural styles; in fact, many want to know the original function of the structures and how the ancient residents went about their daily lives.

After all, humans like to learn about their own kind rather than commune with mute stones.

Interpretive presentations designed primarily to illuminate the activities of the ancient inhabitants can be seen at Tel Dan, a biblical archaeological site located in Upper Galilee (Figs. 9–11). Other possibilities are presented when sites are sheltered; in such instances, objects or replicas can be used particularly effectively. However, while it is true that more techniques can be used on these sites than in open-air ones, such presentations must still be carefully planned and designed. Displaying objects in the precise location in which they were discovered can illustrate the process of excavation, but the practice is not an effective way to interpret the past. Objects or replicas can instead be used to hint at the original function or character of the spaces (Figs. 6, 12). However, the presentation of finds in display cases tends to transform a site into an exhibition hall

Figure 9
Interpretive panel at the main gate, Tel Dan, Israel. This Canaanite royal city was one of the first Israelite settlements in Canaan; it served as an important ceremonial site from the ninth to the seventh century B.C.E. The only information available to assist in interpretation of the site consists of narrative passages from the Bible. The panel, made of metal, incorporates relevant biblical texts.

Figure 10
Stainless steel reconstruction of the altar, Tel Dan.

Figure 11
Housing for holograms, Tel Dan. The relevant biblical narrative passages (see Fig. 9) were not considered sufficient to explain to visitors the importance of a site that does not have any prominent archaeological features other than a large stone bema that was used for sacrifice. This installation, located next to the altar, houses a hologram that illustrates the rites thought to have been performed at the altar.

and—if the material remains uninterpreted—can convey little historical information.

Sites often have large spaces with few or no remains; these places are particularly suited for more creative activities. Some activities include opportunities for visitors to try their hands at ancient craft or production techniques associated with the site.

In spite of the wealth of techniques available today, there are sites that do not lend themselves easily to interpretation—and yet they might have an important story to tell. In such instances, theatrical guides can be effective. Guides can represent the historical period presented; in other cases groups of actors can be stationed along various parts of the visitors' route, reenacting events related to the site. In contrast to traditional tour guides, theatrical guides do not recount the history of a site or explain ruins; instead, they generally speak from ancient texts or deliver addresses that evoke ancient times.

The methods discussed above are just a few examples of the possibilities for presenting and interpreting an archaeological site. The available solutions are as wide-ranging as human imagination and creativity, and new technologies are continually increasing the choices. Even so, regardless of technology, creativity, and innovation, a presentation should not impinge upon the integrity of a site. It is important not only to interpret the past but also to protect the archaeological heritage, leaving it intact for the benefit of future generations.

Figure 12
Restored room in the Herodian Quarter of the Old City, Jerusalem. This Old City site encompasses a residential quarter from the Herodian period, which extended from the first century B.C.E. to the first century C.E. In addition to the original mosaic floor, the restored room contains some reconstructed furniture and objects that were found in situ.

PART TWO

Three Mediterranean Sites

Introduction to Part Two

D URING THE COURSE of the conference, the organizers arranged
visits to three archaeological sites. These were chosen to give the
participants opportunities to consider specific issues relating to
the challenges of management and conservation at complex heritage sites.
The places selected—Piazza Armerina, Knossos, and Ephesus—represent
a range of scientific, aesthetic, historical, and social values. All three locations have acquired considerable economic value by attracting large numbers of visitors. Decisions made over time have, intentionally or not, given
priority to certain values, and the results of the decisions are reflected in
many features of the sites as they are now presented to visitors. During
the conference, the sites were not held up for evaluation but served instead
as examples to provoke thought and discussion about various ways to
resolve significant issues.

As the conference progressed and as the group traveled from
Piazza Armerina to Knossos to Ephesus, the issues under discussion
become more numerous and intricate, reflecting the increasing complexity
of the sites. Piazza Armerina is the location of an important Roman villa,
where the conservation and presentation of the magnificent mosaics have
been given priority in many management decisions; other features, therefore, have played a less prominent role in the presentation. Knossos presents an interesting case of a site reconstructed according to the vision of
one archaeologist. It is now recognized that some of the conjectures that
guided that work early in the century were erroneous and that some of
the interventions are adversely affecting the condition of the original
remains. The reconstruction itself, however, has acquired historical value
and now ranks as an element of significance in the management of the
site. The urban site of Ephesus is among the most important in the
Mediterranean region; as such, its significance is determined by a vast
array of values—scientific and aesthetic, as well as social. Still under excavation, it is visited by more than one million tourists every year. The
management of a site of this magnitude is a complicated undertaking that
must address in a balanced way the preservation of all the elements that
make the site important.

Before each site visit during the conference, participants prepared for the experience by attending an illustrated presentation by an archaeologist on the Getty staff. Each presentation included an account of the main values of the site, a brief history of modern interventions, and a discussion of some of the management issues created by current conditions. In each case particular issues were selected to illustrate some of the most common challenges faced by site managers. These presentations are represented by the following articles.

The Roman Villa at Piazza Armerina, Sicily

Nicholas Stanley-Price

T HE LATE ROMAN VILLA of Piazza Armerina in Sicily is particularly known for its outstanding mosaic floors. Few general surveys
of Roman art and architecture published in the past thirty years
fail to mention the villa. All guidebooks to Sicily and much of the
promotional material for the island's tourism direct the visitor toward
this attraction.

The site is at the locality known as Casale in central southern
Sicily, some four kilometers southwest of the historic town of Piazza
Armerina. At an elevation of 550 meters above sea level, the Villa del
Casale lies at the foot of low hills that are immediately to its north and
east. To the north, the valley of the Nociara River provides some flatland
where it emerges from the hills, but only to the south and southwest does
the landscape open out into extensive vistas of good arable land.

Most of the remains visible today at the Casale site belong to a
late Roman villa constructed probably during the period of 300–330 C.E.
(Ampolo et al. 1971; Kähler 1973). The villa had been preceded by an
earlier villa (known as the Villa Rustica) of the first and second
centuries C.E. Remains have recently been found that indicate an inter-
mediate phase between these two historical episodes, dated to a period
between the second and fourth centuries (De Miro 1988).

Philological evidence appears to link the Roman town site of
Philosophiana, mentioned in the Antonine Itinerary as a way station on the
Catania-Agrigento road, and the Roman remains found at the locality still
known as Sofiana, located six kilometers south of the villa (Adamesteanu
1988). The Villa del Casale has been linked in turn to the existence of this
way station on the principal Roman road in the area.

It is not known how long the Roman villa of the fourth century
remained in use. Ceramics of the Byzantine, Arab, and Norman periods
have been found on the site, together with, in places, associated building
remains. Since the main excavations (by G. V. Gentili) have never been
fully published and since the excavator devoted most of his attention to
the Roman mosaics, it has been necessary to reconstruct the nature of
post-Roman occupation on the site from the few reports available and

from more recent, limited excavations (Ampolo et al. 1971; Wilson 1983; De Miro 1988).

Some reuse of the Roman buildings seems to be attested for the Arabo-Norman period (eleventh to thirteenth centuries), and stray finds suggest activity at the site in the Aragon period (fifteenth to seventeenth centuries). Other finds date from the eighteenth century, by which time the Roman remains are being reported by antiquarians (e.g., Leanti 1761). Some of the Roman villa's walls survive today up to a height of about eight meters, and they have probably always been exposed, even if obscured by woodland and vegetation.

The nonorthogonal plan of the villa is not unusual for large Roman villas (Fig. 1). It has been explained as the result of a single conception with a vanishing point off-site to the north (Ampolo et al. 1971: plan B) or as the result of organization, intentional or not, "around a generalized radial composition of strongly focal character" (MacDonald 1986:274). The ground rises gradually from west to east; the basilica is at the highest point of the excavated area (Fig. 1, no. 58).

The official visitor would presumably have arrived at the monumental entrance of three arches (no. 11a) and, gradually ascending, would have passed through the courtyard (no. 11b), the entrance vestibule (no. 13a), the main peristyle (no. 19), and the great corridor (no. 36b), finally reaching the basilica (no. 58) (Settis 1975).

The villa, built as a single-story building, was constructed primarily of mortared rubble walls faced with irregular pieces of local brownstone. The great majority of excavated floor surfaces consisted of mosaic pavements, half of them figured. The floor of the basilica, in contrast, had a magnificent decoration in opus sectile, while the open courtyards were often paved with brick (see Carandini, Ricci, and De Vos 1982:pl. 32, for the distribution of different types of floor surfaces throughout the site). It is estimated that some thirty-five-hundred square meters of mosaics have been uncovered at the site. In addition, although scarcely mentioned by the main excavator, almost all rooms in the villa buildings had either marble facings or painted frescoes on their walls. Marble statuary would have served as additional decorative elements, but little has survived.

Significance of the Villa at Piazza Armerina

The site of Piazza Armerina has been and continues to be the subject of numerous scholarly studies because of the many unanswered questions about its original owner and precise function. Moreover, with the massive increase in tourism since the Second World War, the site of Piazza Armerina has become widely known to a lay audience. Because of its continuing fascination for scholars and the steadily increasing flow of visitors that it receives, Piazza Armerina presents a number of issues of general relevance for the conservation and management of ancient sites.

The villa has a number of values that together constitute its wider significance. These values can be broadly classified into the categories of

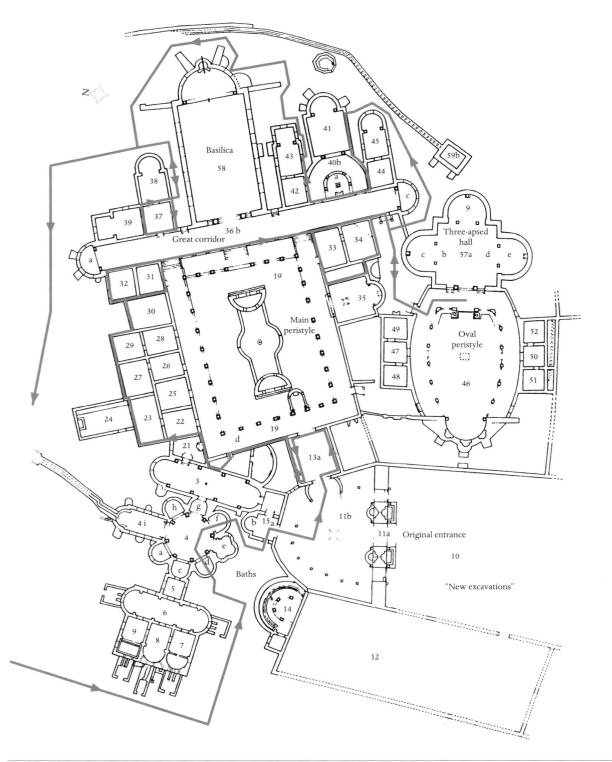

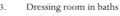

3.	Dressing room in baths	21.	Entrance hall to baths	46.	Oval peristyle
4.	Baths frigidarium	22–26.	Service rooms	57.	Three-apsed hall
11a.	Original entrance	27–30.	Residential apartments	58.	Basilica
11b.	Entrance courtyard	33–34.	Service rooms	59b.	Latrine
13a.	Entrance vestibule	36.	Great corridor	35.	Triclinium
14.	Latrine	37–39.	Apartment of domina		
19.	Main peristyle	40–45.	Apartment of dominus		

Figure 1

Plan of the villa at Piazza Armerina (after Carandini, Ricci, and De Vos 1982). Site elements are
designated numerically; the functions of selected elements are listed in the key above.

(1) historical, (2) aesthetic, (3) scientific, and (4) social and symbolic. The site has also, of course, an economic value and an educational value; these, it might be argued, are derived values, since they depend on those already listed.

Historical value

While the historical value of the Piazza Armerina villa lies partly in its floor mosaics, its primary importance is its contribution to the understanding of late Roman society in Sicily and the Roman Empire. The mosaics constitute one of the largest and most complete series of mosaic floors extant in a late Roman villa (Figs. 2, 3). The subjects depicted provide extensive information about contemporary activities such as hunting and the capture and transport of large animals to the entertainment venues of Rome. In the themes depicted and in the conventions used, they provide important parallels with mosaics found in North Africa. The discoveries at Piazza Armerina are a prime reference point for the student of Roman floor mosaics.

When the villa was first excavated extensively, its size and wealth were quite unexpected for the late Roman period in Sicily. Its value as a unique discovery survived until the excavation, in the 1970s, of two other Roman villas in Sicily. The villas at Patti on the north coast and at Tellaro, south of Syracuse, have proved to be of similar dimensions to that of Piazza Armerina and to have equally fine mosaic floors (Voza 1976–77, 1980–81).

The uniqueness of Piazza Armerina led to arguments in earlier scholarship for an imperial ownership of the villa (e.g., Settis 1975), and if this were the case, its historical value would be exceptional. Following the other villa discoveries in Sicily, however, the ownership of Piazza Armerina is now more often attributed to a Roman of senatorial rank (e.g., Carandini, Ricci, and De Vos 1982). Nevertheless, the existence of a villa as sumptuous as Piazza Armerina in late Roman Sicily—whatever its

Figure 2, below
Detail from the *Labors of Hercules* mosaic in the three-apsed hall (see color plate 1d).

Figure 3, below right
Detail from the *Great Hunt* mosaic in the great corridor. The figure at the lower left has been interpreted as the emperor or the owner of the villa, flanked by two attendants (see color plate 1c).

ownership—was previously unsuspected, and its discovery has required a reinterpretation of the history of this province and its place in the Roman Empire of the time.

Also of historical importance is the philological evidence for connecting the Roman settlement at the locality called Sofiana, south of the villa, with the Philosophiana of the Antonine Itinerary. If this link is valid, and if the villa at Piazza Armerina can be related in the same way, as Carandini's study *Filosofiana* proposes, then the villa's existence is grounded in historical records (Carandini, Ricci, and De Vos 1982).

Aesthetic value

The villa of Piazza Armerina has strong aesthetic value that derives from its location and from the beauty of the mosaic floors. The immediate environment of the villa is unexpectedly verdant, even in summer, for this area of inland Sicily (Fig. 4). The hills that rise above the site from the northeast to the northwest form part of the southern extremity of the Heraean range, which in antiquity was covered in oak forests, as was noted by the classical author Diodorus Siculus (4.84.1). Today the hills are covered with pine, and cypress, oak, eucalyptus, alder, and hazel species are common around the site. The setting, with its wooded hills, shaded valleys, and rich, arable lands to the south, led Cesare Brandi to write of its "Arcadian beauty," reminiscent more of Tuscany than of Sicily (Brandi 1956).

The villa is best known for its beautiful mosaic floors (Figs. 2, 3). Found in relatively good condition, many floors have been lifted and reset, and lacunae have been integrated with ancient tesserae. As a result, for the most part, the floors present complete images for the visitor to appreciate and enjoy.

The protective enclosures erected over the ruins of the villa were designed not only to protect the mosaic floors but also to enhance their aesthetic appeal within an enclosed space. The enclosures, because they

Figure 4
Setting of the villa and its protective enclosures, seen from the southwest. The location of the villa at the foot of wooded hills is an important aesthetic value of the site.

are translucent, allow the verdant surroundings of the site to be glimpsed from inside, thus associating the villa's internal functions with the external world. The design also aimed to convey an impression of the original internal volumes of the Roman structure, thus stimulating the visitor's appreciation of how the villa must once have looked to its occupants.

Scientific value

The villa continues to be the object of numerous scholarly studies as to its original ownership, its historical development, its architecture, and its mosaic floor decoration. Several monographs (Kähler 1973; Carandini, Ricci, and De Vos 1982), many articles, and a number of symposia (e.g., Garraffo 1988) have been dedicated to its study.

These studies reflect both the historic and the scientific value of the villa. The challenges for preservation presented by the excavated villa have given rise to additional scientific investigations. Studies on methods of flood control and on the interior microclimate of the enclosures have been carried out at the villa (Bartolotte and Caputo 1991). The villa also provides an instructive example of the evolution of techniques used in the preservation of floor mosaics since the 1940s, from traditional restoration practices to modern approaches involving documentation, materials analysis, and reversible treatments.

Social and symbolic values

The social and symbolic value of the villa at Piazza Armerina lies principally in the beauty of the mosaics as a source of pride to local inhabitants and to Sicilians in general. The town of Piazza Armerina announces itself as the "Città dei Mosaici," and the local tourism office promotes the villa's mosaics as one of the area's principal attractions. There is, of course, an economic value to the site, in the form of tourism revenue to the local community. This factor should not be overemphasized, however, since most of the tourism is transient, and many visitors include the site as part of a day's excursion without spending time (and therefore money) in the town of Piazza Armerina. Even so, the local sale of souvenirs with motifs from the mosaics is a well-developed business. At the regional level, as a tourist attraction, Piazza Armerina joins other sites in Sicily such as Agrigento, Selinunte, and Segesta in the promotional literature and other media.

Another important social value lies in the depiction of Roman life and leisure in the mosaic floors of the villa. Nonspecialist visitors can immediately identify with many of the scenes represented—the "bikini girls" mosaic being only the most obvious example. Whatever the relationship between today's reality and that of the Roman past, the visitor's tendency to associate the two suggests an empathy with the past that is the first step toward an enhanced appreciation of the cultural heritage.

Since values are ascribed to places rather than being inherent in them, a list of values of the Roman villa at Piazza Armerina would have been different if drawn up forty years ago by those concerned with the excavation and preservation of the remains. The difference in point of view is highlighted below in the discussion of issues raised by interventions at the villa. Moreover, the solutions adopted for protection of the villa have at times revealed a conflict, or at least an incompatibility, between the values that were to be preserved.

History of Interventions

The villa has been subject to a series of interventions (excavation, restoration, protection) since its modern rediscovery (see chronological outline, p. 74). The major part of the remains of the villa visible today were excavated by Cultrera and Gentili in the 1940s and 1950s. Efforts to protect the excavated remains started with the reburial policy followed by Pappalardo in 1881 and then evolved toward the erection of protective roofs and enclosures over remains left visible after excavation (Pappalardo 1881:173ff.). Modern interventions have consisted of small-scale excavations (to resolve specific questions raised by earlier investigations) and of conservation work that addressed problems caused by earlier treatments and by a natural disaster, the flooding of the site in 1991.

In 1881 Pappalardo appears to have begun excavations in areas where ancient walls were visible above ground level: the entrance gate (Fig. 1, no. 11a), the basilica (no. 58), and the three-apsed hall (no. 57). A trench was also opened in the oval peristyle (no. 46). Pappalardo's decision to dig in the area of the three-apsed hall was determined by reports of buried mosaics previously discovered and destroyed by treasure hunters. A four-by-four-meter trench in the southeast corner of the central hall (no. 57a) uncovered part of the *Labors of Hercules* mosaic at a depth of 2.10 meters.

Suspecting the presence of a late Roman villa, Orsi dedicated two years (1929–30) to the Villa del Casale in an attempt to explain the presence of the large-scale mosaics uncovered by Pappalardo. Orsi and Carta reopened and enlarged the Pappalardo trench in the three-apsed hall, uncovering an eight-by-eight-meter area of the *Labors of Hercules* mosaic (Orsi 1934).

In 1935 new funding made it possible for Cultrera to launch a new project of excavation aimed at gradually uncovering the villa that was now proved to exist and leaving the remains permanently exposed. After three campaigns (1935–37), which lowered the level of the archaeological deposit by five meters without producing immediate results, Cultrera, in 1938–40, completely exposed the floor plan of the three-apsed hall. In 1940–43 he went on to uncover the eastern half of the oval peristyle (Fig. 1, no. 46), as well as rooms 49 and 36c and the walls of room 35. At the same time, having decided on visible preservation of the mosaics, Cultrera had Piero Gazzola design and erect a roof over the three-apsed hall (Gentili 1966:pl. 1; Carandini, Ricci, and De Vos 1982:endpapers).

In 1942–43 the mosaics in the three-apsed hall (now roofed) were restored. Most sections were lifted, set on new cement bases, and fixed to the floor with numerous iron pins. Lacunae were filled in with cement, and the mosaics were cleaned with pumice. However, several of the lifted mosaics were not replaced in situ for lack of funds. Severe problems involving loss of cohesion of the tesserae had been caused by visitors and guides throwing hydrochloric acid on the mosaics to remove encrustation and make them more legible (Bernabò Brea 1947). Conservation work on the mosaics continued from 1942 to 1949, although it was interrupted in 1943 with the landing of the Allies in Sicily. The Allied Military Command, through its Subcommission on Monuments, Fine Arts, and Archives, made the continuation of the work possible in 1944.

The extensive excavations by Gentili started in 1950, when he uncovered most of the south wing of the villa, taking advantage of Cultrera's having lowered the level of the archaeological deposit. The renewed work at the site was this time at the initiative of the Comune of Piazza Armerina, with public funding from the regional government of Sicily. Gentili then moved north to expose the remaining part of the villa as seen today (Figs. 5, 6). While the first plan of the completely exposed villa was published by Gentili in 1956, it is dated 1953—which gives an idea of how fast Gentili cleared the archaeological deposit covering the north section of the villa (Gentili 1956).

Since Gentili's excavations, two attempts have been made to recover stratigraphic information to further the understanding of the occupation sequence on the Casale site. In 1970 Carandini opened several test trenches in the main peristyle, baths, and basilica and managed to date

Figure 5, below
Entrance vestibule and peristyle of the villa before the construction of the enclosures. The wooden planks served as walkways to protect the mosaics.

Figure 6, below right
South wing of the central peristyle after the re-erection of columns and before the construction of the protective enclosures. The peristyle garden has since been replanted.

securely the construction of the late Roman villa to 300–320 c.e. All previous structures had been leveled to prepare the site for the new palatial villa built on four different levels. The bath complex was built on the same alignment as a previous bath building belonging to the first-century Villa Rustica or to a second-century phase of it (Ampolo et al. 1971).

The second series of renewed excavations was carried out between 1983 and 1988 by the Soprintendenza Archeologica of Agrigento, directed by Ernesto De Miro and Graziella Fiorentini. They provided firm evidence for the phases of occupation before and after the construction of the late imperial villa (De Miro 1988).

The renewed excavations by Carandini in 1970 were undertaken within the villa's core area, where the protective enclosures designed by architect Franco Minissi were already in place. Minissi's protective enclosures, still present today, consist of a lightweight metal skeleton sheathed with translucent panels of plastic (Fig. 7).[1] Minissi aimed "to form anew (not reconstruct) the room-areas corresponding to the different mosaics" using only material that was obviously new. His intent was to protect the mosaics from the weather while retaining maximum light and enabling visitors to see all the mosaics without walking upon them (Minissi 1961:131).

Since the erection of the protective enclosures in the late 1950s, conservation interventions have addressed maintenance and materials

Figure 7
Aerial view of the villa from the southwest, showing the extent of the protective enclosures. The large roof in the center background (covering the basilica), deliberately omitted in Minissi's design, was not built until 1977. The line of an aqueduct cuts the slope of the hill above the villa buildings.

Chronological outline of use, rediscovery, and modern intervention for the Roman Villa del Casale at Piazza Armerina. Excluded are ancient interventions, such as repairs to mosaic floors, and the reuse in Norman times of Roman structures, as well as antiquarian references to the presumed site of the villa.

1881	L. Pappalardo digs for mosaics in area of three-apsed hall (Fig. 1, no. 57) and at main entrance (no. 11a). Trenches backfilled. Pappalardo makes report to Comune of Piazza Armerina (Pappalardo 1881).
1929–30	P. Orsi and R. Carta excavate three-apsed hall (no. 57) and a necropolis on Mount Mangone, immediately to the north of the villa. Much publicity given to mosaic finds, which are reburied (Orsi 1934).
1935–45	G. Cultrera completes clearance of three-apsed hall, oval peristyle (no. 46), and part of corridor (no. 36c). P. Gazzola erects protective roof over three-apsed hall. Mosaics lifted and restored (Cultrera 1936, 1940; Bernabò Brea 1947).
1950–54	G. V. Gentili clears rest of villa that is visible today. Long report on first two campaigns (Gentili 1950, 1952a, 1952b); otherwise most of work unpublished. Further mosaic consolidation; columns re-erected and restored.
1957–60	F. Minissi constructs protective enclosure and walkways; some wall rebuilding required. All mosaics after restoration protected with roofs. Basilica (no. 58) remains exposed. Artificial lighting system installed. Site opened to visitors (Minissi 1961).
1970	C. Ampolo, A. Carandini, G. Pucci, and P. Pensabene excavate test trenches to retrieve stratigraphic data (Ampolo et al. 1971).
1972	E. De Miro and F. Minissi propose site museum in town of Piazza Armerina (not realized) (De Miro and Minissi 1972). Soprintendente G. Voza undertakes conservation measures: upslope water diversion channel; substitution of deteriorated material on Minissi's protective roof (Soprintendenza 1994).
1977	Soprintendenza undertakes roofing of basilica (omitted by Minissi) (Soprintendenza 1994).
1982–88	Soprintendenza improves site drainage; substitutes materials on Minissi's protective roof (Soprintendenza 1994).
1983–88	Soprintendenza conducts "new excavations" in 1983 (E. De Miro) and in 1986–88 (G. Fiorentini) in area southwest of villa entrance, to check villa phases. 1983 campaign published (De Miro 1988).
1987	Regional conservation center, Palermo, makes proposals for mosaics conservation (Soprintendenza 1994).
1991	Regional conservation center, Palermo, conducts study of microclimatic conditions at site (Bartolotte and Caputo 1991). Soprintendenza conducts emergency treatment of mosaics, wall paintings, and opus sectile floor following flood of villa due to poor drainage (Scognamiglio 1992a, 1992b; Soprintendenza 1994).
1992	Soprintendenza conducts conservation project on villa wall paintings (Soprintendenza 1994).
1993–95	Soprintendenza conserves opus sectile floor of basilica and mosaics in three-apsed hall and other rooms of villa.

replacement for the enclosures, deterioration of the mosaic floors and wall paintings, and damage caused by flooding (see chronological outline, p. 74).

The most urgent intervention followed the extensive flooding of the villa site on 13 October 1991, when exceptionally heavy rains throughout southern Italy caused widespread damage. The whole villa was inundated with water and mud to a depth of up to half a meter. The regional conservation center in Palermo undertook emergency cleaning of the mosaics and submitted a report with wide-ranging recommendations for improving site drainage, for documenting all previous interventions, for consolidating the mosaics, and for removing the protective enclosures because of the adverse microclimates they created (Scognamiglio 1992a, 1992b). Some of these recommendations concerning the mosaics and wall paintings have since been implemented.

Issues Raised by the Interventions

The various interventions (excavation, conservation, protection, and so on) over the past one hundred years have raised a number of issues. These, or similar issues, are relevant to a large number of archaeological sites in the Mediterranean region. Many of these issues can be classified into four problem areas: (1) distortion of our understanding of an ancient site by the dominant research interests of previous investigators; (2) the protection of mosaics in situ through roofing; (3) the design of translucent enclosure buildings for ancient remains; and (4) the design of visitor itineraries that—while compatible with conservation objectives—successfully inform the visitor.

Distortion of our understanding of an ancient site by the dominant research interests of previous investigators

Helped by the clearance of the deep overlying deposit by the preceding excavator, Cultrera, Gentili was able to expose a large series of outstanding floor mosaics in a relatively short time. As a result, the villa at Piazza Armerina has become famous to scholars and visitors alike for its mosaics. For both groups, however, the excavator's concentration on the floor mosaics resulted in the loss of most of the ancillary information that would assist in understanding their context. A scholarly publication of the many campaigns of excavation work has not appeared; nor are most of the movable finds from the excavations available for study.

The site of the Villa del Casale is usually viewed today as a single-phase Roman villa—whereas it is known that it featured several phases of occupation and reoccupation into the medieval period. Reconstructions (from reports and visible remains on site) of the subsequent phases of occupation (Wilson 1983:fig. 23) show how much was discarded during the leveling of the archaeological deposit to reach the mosaic floors.

One central issue raised by the main excavations at the villa is the importance of documenting and publishing all excavated material and subsequent interventions. While records of earlier interventions are today often found to be inadequate, it is nevertheless necessary to understand the climate of thought regarding scholarship and preservation that prevailed at the time. It is also important to retrieve as much information as possible that was overlooked in the past because of research priorities that differed from those of today; Carandini and coworkers have done this for the villa (Carandini, Ricci, and De Vos 1982). Since knowledge about sites and historical information evolve over time, visitors to ancient sites must be told how information about them is acquired and how the visible remains might present a picture that does not reflect past realities.

Protection of mosaics in situ through roofing

The roof erected over the three-apsed hall in 1941–42 consisted of a wooden frame covered with clay tiles supported by massive brick pillars (Fig. 8) (Gentili 1966:pl. 1; Carandini, Ricci, and De Vos 1982:endpapers). The curvilinear walls of the building were restored in part to help support the new pillars. The design was later criticized by Cesare Brandi, who thought it made what should be a sumptuous room look like a hayloft. The visitors could see the mosaics only by walking on them or by climbing a wooden observation tower built at the entrance to the shelter (Brandi 1956). Gazzola's roof covered the outstanding mosaics of the three-apsed hall, but with the continuation of excavations, many more mosaics were exposed and required protection.

The construction of Gazzola's roof in the 1940s raises important questions concerning the protection of floor mosaics in situ. How can protective roofs or shelters be designed to protect mosaics from the weather while also allowing them to be easily seen? Can a new roof be designed that does not have an adverse aesthetic impact on the site— by dominating the landscape, for instance?

Furthermore, when continued excavation reveals many additional areas requiring protection, the first roof erected may need

Figure 8
Protective roof (in background) constructed over the three-apsed hall in 1941–42 by Piero Gazzola. The roof was later demolished when Minissi's protective enclosures were built in the late 1950s. The mosaic floors are covered with sand for protection.

Figure 9
Protective enclosure of the vestibule seen from the northwest. Wall panels of sheet glass, which have replaced the original corrugated plastic sheathing material, have encouraged heat buildup.

Figure 10
Protective enclosure over the three-apsed hall. The original corrugated plastic sheathing material has been replaced with sheet glass. The false ceiling can be clearly seen (cf. Fig. 12).

to be reconsidered or even demolished (as was the case with Gazzola's roof). Should "first" roofs be deliberately designed to be low in cost and easily dismantled?

Design of translucent enclosure buildings for ancient remains

The protective enclosure buildings designed by Minissi were intended to protect the mosaics while also allowing visitors optimal viewing (Figs. 9, 10) (Stanley-Price and Ponti 1996). These separate aims required some compromises in the design that allowed the reconciliation of technical conservation requirements and aesthetic considerations.

On the conservation side, in order to avoid the potential heat problem (a "greenhouse effect") posed by a translucent structure in the Sicilian

Figure 11, above
Glass louvers for ventilation of the protective enclosures. The louvers are one of a series of measures for reducing heat buildup inside the protective enclosures. These measures have had only partial success.

Figure 12, right
False ceiling made of plastic panels, designed to help reduce heat buildup. These ceilings also suggest the original internal volumes of the rooms of the villa, as seen here in the octagonal frigidarium in the baths (Fig. 1, no. 4).

climate, Minissi proposed to air-condition the structure; no funds were available, however, to implement this proposal. Despite a number of design features to reduce heat transmission (Figs. 11, 12), the heat buildup inside the two enclosures (the main peristyle area and the separate three-apsed hall enclosure) can at times be intense. The resulting high temperatures can be intolerable to visitors, who have been known to faint.

As for the archaeological remains, the absolute high values and, especially, the daily and seasonal fluctuations of temperature and relative humidity are likely to contribute to deterioration (Scognamiglio 1992b). Even so, it can be argued that the villa's mosaics are in much better condition today, after forty years of enclosure, than if they had been left exposed to the elements.

From the point of view of aesthetic presentation, Minissi's design aimed to convey an impression to visitors of the interior volumes of rooms containing mosaics and to allow visitors to see the mosaics without walking on them. The use of a translucent enclosure material led to the problem of shadows falling across the mosaics, despite measures taken by Minissi to avoid this effect (Fig. 13). Moreover, the translucent material allows plenty of natural light to illuminate the mosaics—arguably much more than they would have originally received. The strong natural illumination of the mosaics and the system of walkways enabling the spectator to gaze downward at them appear to be so successful that few visitors look upward at the recreated volumes of the enclosure building (Fig. 14).

Figure 13, above
Shadows cast by the corrugated plastic side panels installed by Minissi in the 1950s. Minissi aimed to provide maximum light for viewing of the mosaics and to avoid the casting of shadows on them. His solution was not fully successful. The consolidated wall that supports the visitor walkway can also be seen.

Figure 14, above right
Metal walkways that allow visitors to view the mosaics without walking on them. These walkways—installed in the 1950s—are still in use today and cannot easily accommodate large numbers of visitors at peak periods. The false ceiling above and the sheet glass wall panels filter the midmorning sun unevenly.

The translucent enclosures at Piazza Armerina raise questions regarding conservation, cost, and aesthetics. From the conservation point of view, the risk of creating a greenhouse effect by enclosing ancient remains within a translucent structure is a serious one. In exacerbating temperature and relative humidity fluctuations, this type of solution can promote cycles of expansion and contraction of materials (potentially damaging particularly where original and new materials are in contact) and cycles of crystallization and dissolution of soluble salts. This risk can be attenuated by the installation of well-designed climate control systems. The costs of climate control need to be considered along with the replacement costs of the materials of the protective structure (in this case, plastics).

As for aesthetics, this type of solution offers opportunities to design a structure that is aesthetically compatible with the environment of the ancient remains and that re-creates some idea of the original volumes of the enclosed spaces. The solution employed at the villa raises other important questions concerning appropriate light levels for viewing ancient mosaic floors and the best way for mosaics to be seen without being walked upon. These questions—which essentially ask whether the modern visitor experience should mimic original conditions of the site—are further developed below.

Design of visitor itineraries that—while compatible with conservation objectives—successfully inform the visitor

The system of raised walkways, which rest upon the consolidated wall tops of the villa's rooms, enables visitors to see all the mosaics without walking upon them (Fig. 14). The protective enclosure suggests to some extent the original interior volumes of the rooms containing mosaics, though it is uncertain whether many visitors appreciate this point (Fig. 15).

Figure 15
Supports of the protective enclosures
designed to suggest the interior volumes of
the original building (see also Fig. 14). Here,
at the northwest angle of the main peristyle,
the support also represents the form of a column capital. Minissi's aim was "to form anew
(not reconstruct) the room-areas corresponding to the different mosaics" (Minissi
1961:131).

Both of these goals influenced Minissi's original design. With the benefit
of hindsight and with today's changing perspectives, the solution adopted
in the 1950s raises a number of issues concerning visitor access and
interpretation.

The modern visitor can view all the preserved floors that have
been uncovered—more, in fact, than a Roman visitor to the villa would
probably have seen. However, the aesthetic presentation of the
outstanding floor mosaics is achieved at the expense of an accurate
historical interpretation of how a Roman villa functioned. The fixed
visitor route follows the wall tops of a series of rooms; however, by
so doing, it cannot simulate original patterns of movement in the
ancient villa.

In recent years, visitors, instead of arriving through the
monumental entrance of the villa (Fig. 1, no. 11a), have arrived from the
north on a route that takes them past the furnaces of the bath complex
and a latrine (no. 14)—hardly the approach that a distinguished Roman
visitor would have taken. The peristyle, around which Roman inhabitants
and visitors would have walked, can be viewed only from afar by the
visitor; so too the important basilica.

To understand the villa, visitors must depend on information
from a guidebook or from the tour guides who escort groups. (The official

Figure 16
Crowds of midmorning visitors at the villa in May 1995. The fixed itinerary created by the walkways built in the 1950s is no longer adequate to serve the number of visitors—as many as two thousand per day at peak periods.

English-language guidebook is Gentili's [1966].) There is almost no written or visual information provided on the site—information that might, for instance, illuminate the functions of the rooms.

The priority given to aesthetic presentation of the mosaics over the simulation of original routes of movement through the villa is understandable given Minissi's aim to create a "special kind of museum round exhibits which were already in place" (Minissi 1961:131). Moreover, many historical questions—even the functions of several rooms—remain unresolved, and so relatively little information can be presented to the visitor with confidence. Another issue raised by the fixed visitor route within the main enclosure—one that could not be foreseen by the decision makers of the 1950s—is the carrying capacity of the walkways. As a result of the advent of mass tourism (Fig. 16), at peak periods, the opportunity to experience the mosaics—carefully designed by Minissi and his colleagues—is at risk of being lost in a single-file mass surge of visitors toward the only exit.

In summary, the protective enclosures constructed at the villa forty years ago raise some general issues for site management today. Foremost of these is the reconciliation of conservation and presentation objectives in a site management plan. Both aesthetic and historical values need to be incorporated into the presentation of floor mosaics (or any decorative surfaces). Open questions are whether the design of modern visitor itineraries should mimic the probable access patterns of the original occupants of the site, and whether the viewing conditions of, for example, ancient mosaics should attempt to imitate original conditions or should instead be optimized for the convenience of the modern-day visitor. Finally, the need to accommodate today's mass tourism emphasizes the necessity of upgrading visitor facilities designed several decades ago.

Others have argued that the protective enclosure and visitor itinerary designed forty years ago should now be considered obsolete, since they cause damage to the site's remains and provide an unsatisfactory visitor experience. If so, the many issues that this solution attempted to resolve in the 1950s are no less immediate today—both for Piazza Armerina and for ancient sites in general.

Acknowledgments

The author owes a particular debt to Dr. Gianni Ponti, who researched the history of interventions at the villa, facilitated local liaison in Italy, and accompanied the author on research visits to Piazza Armerina for the preparation of this study. The author is also indebted to Dr. Gianfillipo Villari, *soprintendente* of the Soprintendenza ai Beni Culturali e Ambientali di Enna, for much help and for allowing access to unpublished reports in the soprintendenza's archives; and to other members of the staff who helped provide information about the villa: Dr. Enza Cilia Platamone, the architect Rosa Oliva, Dr. Anna Bombaci, the architect Claudio Meraglia, and the surveyor Liborio Bellone. In Rome, the architect Franco Minissi was very helpful in discussing his work at the villa, as was Professor Andrea Carandini. The author is grateful to all those mentioned for helping make this study possible.

Note

1. Perspex, manufactured by ICI of the United Kingdom.

References

Adamesteanu, D.
1988   Sofiana: Scavi, 1954 e 1961. In *La villa romana del Casale di Piazza Armerina: Atti della IV Riunione Scientifica della Scuola di Perfezionamento in Archeologia Classica dell'Università di Catania*, ed. Salvatore Garraffo, 74–83. Cronache di Archeologia, vol. 23. Catania: Istituto di Archeologia, Università di Catania.

Ampolo C., A. Carandini, G. Pucci, and P. Pensabene
1971   La Villa del Casale a Piazza Armerina: Problemi, saggi stratigrafici ed altre ricerche. *Mélanges de l'Ecole Française de Rome, Antiquité* 83:141–281.

Bartolotte, A., and V. Caputo
1991   Piazza Armerina—villa romana del Casale: Indagine microclimatica. Laboratorio di Fisica, Centro Regionale per la Progettazione e il Restauro, Palermo.

Bernabò Brea, L.
1947   Piazza Armerina: Restauri dei mosaici romani del Casale. *Notizie degli Scavi di Antichità*, 252–53.

Brandi, C.
1956   Archeologia siciliana. *Bollettino dell'Istituto Centrale del Restauro* 27–28:93–100.

Carandini, A., A. Ricci, and M. De Vos
1982   *Filosofiana: The Villa of Piazza Armerina.* 2 vols. Palermo: S. F. Flaccovio.

Cultrera, G.
1936   Scavi, scoperte e restauri di monumenti antichi in Sicilia nel quinquennio 1931–1935. *Atti della Società Italiana per il Progresso delle Scienze* 2(3):612.

1940   Sicilia, Piazza Armerina: Notiziario di scavi, scoperte, studi relativi all'Impero Romano. *Bollettino Comunale di Roma* 68:129–30.

De Miro, E.

1988   La Villa del Casale di Piazza Armerina: Nuove ricerche. In *La villa romana del Casale di Piazza Armerina: Atti della IV Riunione Scientifica della Scuola di Perfezionamento in Archeologia Classica dell'Università di Catania,* ed. Salvatore Garraffo, 58–72. Cronache di Archeologia, vol. 23. Catania: Istituto di Archeologia, Università di Catania.

De Miro, E., and E. F. Minissi

1972   Progetto per il Museo di Piazza Armerina. *Musei e gallerie d'Italia* 17.

Garraffo, S., ed.

1988   *La villa romana del Casale di Piazza Armerina. Atti della IV Riunione Scientifica della Scuola di Perfezionamento in Archeologia Classica dell'Università di Catania.* Cronache di Archeologia, vol. 23. Catania: Istituto di Archeologia, Università di Catania.

Gentili, G. V.

1950   Piazza Armerina: Grandiosa villa romana in contrada Casale. *Notizie degli Scavi di Antichità,* 291–335.

1952a   La villa romana del Casale di Piazza Armerina. In *Atti del I Congresso Nazionale di Archeologia Cristiana, Siracusa, 19–24 settembre 1950,* 171–82. Rome: "L'Erma" di Bretschneider.

1952b   I mosaici della villa romana del Casale di Piazza Armerina. *Bollettino d'Arte* 37:33–46.

1956   La villa imperiale di Piazza Armerina. In *Atti del VII Congresso Nazionale di Storia dell'Architettura, 24–30 settembre 1950,* 247–50. Palermo: Il Comitato.

1966   *The Imperial Villa of Piazza Armerina.* Guidebooks to the Museums, Galleries, and Monuments of Italy, no. 87. 3d English edition. Rome: Istituto Poligrafico dello Stato, Libreria dello Stato.

Kähler, H.

1973   *Die Villa des Maxentius bei Piazza Armerina.* Monumenta Artis Romanae, vol. 12. Berlin: Mann.

Leanti, A.

1761   *Lo stato presente della Sicilia.* Palermo: Francesco Valenza Impressore della Ss. Crociata.

MacDonald, W. L.

1986   The Piazza Armerina villa. Appendix to *The Architecture of the Roman Empire.* Vol. 2, *An Urban Appraisal,* 274–83. New Haven, Conn.: Yale University Press.

Minissi, F.

1961   Protection of the mosaic pavements of the Roman villa at Piazza Armerina. *Museum* 14:131–32.

Orsi, P.

1934   Romanità e avanzi romani in Sicilia: Piazza Armerina. *Roma* 12:255.

Pappalardo, L.

1881   *Le recenti scoperte in contrada Casale presso Piazza Armerina.* N.p.

Scognamiglio, M.

1992a   Emergency intervention on flooded mosaics at Piazza Armerina. *International Committee for the Conservation of Mosaics Newsletter* 9:17–18.

1992b   Piazza Armerina: Villa romana del Casale. Centro Regionale per la Progettazione e il Restauro, Palermo.

Settis, S.

1975   Per l'interpretazione di Piazza Armerina. *Mélanges de l'École Française de Rome* 87:873–994.

Soprintendenza ai Beni Culturali e Ambientali di Enna

1994   Interview by author, Enna, Italy, March–September.

Stanley-Price, N. P., and G. Ponti

1996   Protective enclosures for mosaic floors: A review of Piazza Armerina, Sicily, after forty years. Paper presented at the Sixth Conference of the International Committee for the Conservation of Mosaics, 24–28 October, in Nicosia, Cyprus.

Voza, G.

1976–77   La villa romana del Tellaro. *Kokalos* 22–23:572–73.

1980–81   Villa romana di Patti. *Kokalos* 26–27:690–93.

Wilson, R. J. A.

1983   *Piazza Armerina*. London: Granada Publishing.

1a

1b

Plates 1a–d
Roman villa of Piazza Armerina, Sicily, Italy.
The general view of the baths (a) shows the
enclosures erected to protect the site's mosaic
floors, which are among the most complete in
a late Roman villa. The *Great Hunt* mosaic
(b, c) is protected by roofing and is viewed
both from ground level and from an elevated
walkway. The *Labors of Hercules* mosaic,
shown in detail (d), is another of the villa's
most important artworks.

1d

88

2a

Plates 2a–d
The palace of Knossos, Crete, Greece, excavated and reconstructed by Arthur Evans beginning in 1900. The North Lustral Basin (a) and its restored internal columns (b) show how modern structures now dominate the site. The original Griffin Fresco, very little of which was actually preserved, was "restored" in 1913, and three copies (c) were later added around the Throne Room. These frescoes, like the copy of the Cupbearer Fresco (d) in the South Propylaeum, as well as the rest of the palace, are largely modern creations.

2b

2c

2d

3a

Plates 3a–e

Ephesus, Turkey. The Greco-Roman city of
Ephesus (a), seen from Mount Coressus; in
center foreground is the upper ancient city;
the modern town of Selçuk is seen in the
distance. Ephesus retains its integrity as an
ancient landscape and as an example of
Hellenistic and Roman architecture and urban
planning. The restored Library of Celsus (b)
is the site's most prominent structure; other
remains (c) evoke the romantic pastoral
quality of ruins overgrown by nature. The
enigmatic tumble of architectural pieces in
Domitian Square (d) both confuses and
intrigues visitors, while the monumental
theater (e), recently restored, today occasionally serves as an entertainment venue, pending a final decision on its conservation and
future use.

3b

3c

92

3d

3e

Knossos

John K. Papadopoulos

IN 1900 ARTHUR JOHN EVANS embarked on a full-scale excavation at the prehistoric site on the Kephala Hill at Knossos and immediately came across the remains of the building he was to call the Palace of Minos (Figs. 1–4).[1] The discovery, later referred to as "the find of a lifetime" (Horwitz 1981; Evans 1943; Harden 1983), brought to light a hitherto-unknown civilization, dubbed the Minoan. Early in this century, Evans not only excavated the site but boldly transformed the monument—through restoration, reconstruction, and reinforced concrete—into one of the most frequently visited archaeological sites in the Old World.

The original Neolithic settlement, probably dating to before 7000 B.C.E., as well as the later palace at Knossos, are situated on the low hill of Kephala, approximately five kilometers southeast of Heraklion (Candia).[2] The greater archaeological area of Knossos (Fig. 2), as defined by Hood and Smyth (1981:1), is significantly larger than the immediate palace site; it covers an area of some ten square kilometers, being just under five kilometers north to south, with a maximum width of three kilometers east to west.[3] This area includes the settlement site of Knossos, in its various phases, as well as most of the cemeteries of all periods. Only a small portion of this area is exposed today as part of the archaeological site; this portion includes, in addition to privately owned plots of agricultural land, six modern villages.[4] Intensive building in recent years has transformed the northern part of the area into a suburb of Heraklion. Nevertheless, it has been remarked that "perhaps no other region of ancient settlement in Greece has been so thoroughly explored as this area of some ten square kilometers" (Hood and Smyth 1981:1).

As a large settlement and cemetery site of many periods, Knossos raises a variety of issues and shares many of the problems inherent at all sites with a long and continuous occupation history. At the same time, despite almost a century of excavation and study, the site is best known, among both specialists and the broader public, for its remarkable central building, conventionally called a palace (Fig. 3) (Graham 1962; Cadogan 1976; Hägg and Marinatos 1987; cf. Castleden 1990). This building, discovered early in the history of investigations at the site and extensively explored, is one of the earliest ancient buildings to have been restored to

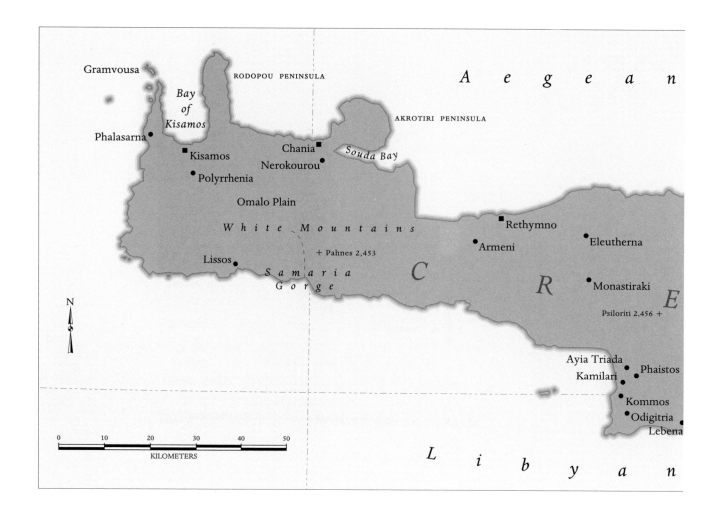

Figure 1
Map of Crete showing locations of
major sites.

such a scale and extent, particularly to the level of the upper stories.[5]
The work on its restoration was commenced immediately after the epoch-
making discoveries of its excavator. Indeed, the excavation, interpretation,
and restoration of the palace are inseparable from the work and vision of
Evans—so much so that his restoration has itself assumed historical
importance.

Significance of Knossos

The site of Knossos, and more particularly the Bronze Age palace, has
great significance, as well as current relevance, as seen from various perspectives. The importance of the site derives primarily, of course, from the
many spectacular finds made there, but beyond that, Knossos has a large
role in the local, national, and popular image, as well as a strong economic
impact on the region.

Historical value

Because it brought to light a hitherto-unknown prehistoric civilization,
Knossos has a strong historical value. It is the site of one of the earliest
complex societies in Europe—one that enjoyed extensive foreign relations,
not only with the Greek mainland but also, in particular, with the Near
East and Egypt. In addition, the excavations at Knossos have yielded abun-

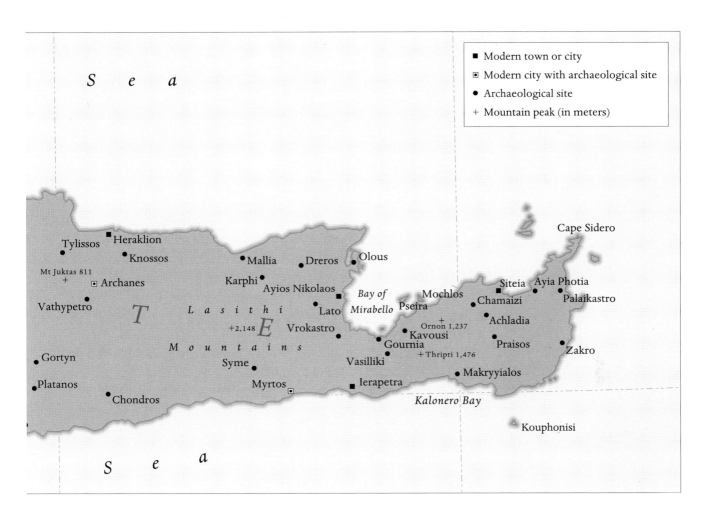

dant evidence of advanced technology in various materials; they have also brought to light the earliest known syllabic script in the Aegean (Linear A) and the earliest verified written Greek (Linear B). Knossos is the earliest and largest Neolithic site on Crete and one of the earliest permanent settlements on any of the Mediterranean islands. It has also been a large urban nucleus in various periods from the Bronze Age, beginning perhaps as early as the later third millennium B.C.E., through the early Iron Age, and into the Classical, Hellenistic, and Roman periods. There are also important remains spanning the Byzantine period up to the Arab conquest of Crete (ca. 827 C.E.), at which time Heraklion became the capital of the island. Although the settlement at Knossos was at its most extensive during the Palatial period of the Bronze Age, during the late Hellenistic period, and, again, during early Roman times, it was an important settlement for an exceptionally long period of time—at least seven thousand years (Evely, Hughes-Brock, and Momigliano 1994).

Scientific value

The historical significance of the site gives Knossos great scientific value as the type site of Minoan culture and one of the cornerstones for the traditional chronology of the Aegean and parts of the eastern Mediterranean in the Bronze Age. The palace and its surrounds have been the object of

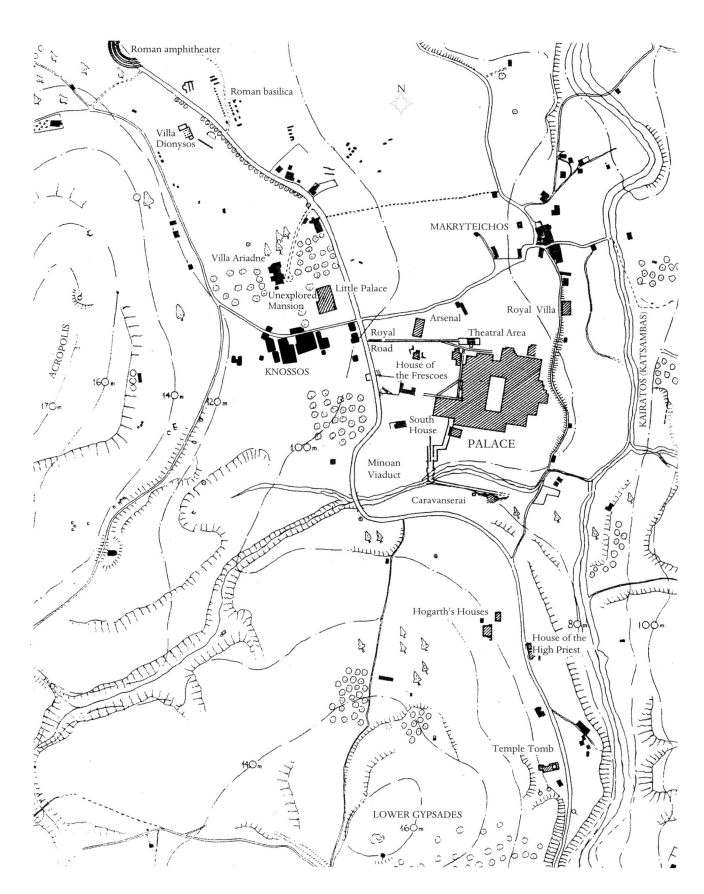

Figure 2

Part of the greater area of the archaeological
site of Knossos, showing some of the more
prominent remains outside the palace.

Figure 3
Plan of the palace of Knossos (after A. Evans).

A–C West Magazines
I–XVIII West Magazines
1. Kouloures
2, 2′. Altars
3. West Porch
4–11. Corridor of the Procession
5. Southwest Porch
6. Stepped Portico
7. South Terrace
8, 8′. South Propylaeum
9. South Corridor
10. South Porch
11. Priest King Relief
12. Site of the Greek temple
13. Bathtub with Linear B Tablets
14. Long Corridor of the West
    Magazines
15. Deposit of Hieroglyphic Tablets
16. Corridor of the Stone Basin
17. Anteroom of the Throne Room

18. Throne Room
19. Inner Sanctuary
20. Stepped Porch
21. Tripartite Shrine
22. Lobby of the Stone Seat
23. Temple Repositories
24. Pillar Crypts
25. Grand Staircase
26. Hall of the Double Axes (King's Hall)
27. Queen's Hall
28. Queen's Dressing Room
29. Court of the Distaffs
30. Service Staircase
31. Southeast Bathroom
32. Shrine of the Double Axes
33. Southeast Lustral Basin
34. Lobby of the Wooden Posts
35. East Portico
36. Lapidary's Workshop
37. Schoolroom

38. Court of the Stone Spout
39. Magazines of the Giant Pithoi
40. East Bastion
41. Corridor of the Draughtboard
42. Northeast Hall
43. Northeast Magazines
44. Room of the Stone Drainhead
45. Magazine of the Medallion Pithoi
46. Corridor of the Bays
47. Early Keep
48. North Entrance Passage
49. North Pillar Hall
50. North Gate
51. North Lustral Basin and Initiatory Area
52. Northwest Portico
53. Theatral Area
54. Royal Road
55. Northwest Entrance?

Figure 4
Knossos viewed from the east in 1902, two years after Evans started his excavations. The soil dumps on the eastern slopes of the site, which were visible in 1901, have been moved. The Throne Room has been roofed (see Fig. 7), a retaining wall for the Central Court has been built, and various parts of the Domestic Quarter have been partially restored or consolidated.

prolific scholarly research in many areas—including archaeological, historical, philological, art-historical, anthropological, and scientific—both for the Bronze Age and for earlier and later periods.

Symbolic and associative values

Crete is the setting for numerous Greek myths, and of these, many are enacted against the elaborate backdrop of the palace of Knossos. The symbolic and associative values of the site have defied the passage of time to such an extent that although Minoan Knossos was lost from human view, it was never lost from human memory. The legendary Minos, son of Zeus and Europa, featured prominently in later Greek accounts as the first person to organize a navy, through which he controlled the greater part of the Aegean, where he also established the first colonies;[6] he lived on even in death as one of the great judges of the underworld (Bažant 1992:570–74). Pasiphaë, the Minotaur, and Daidalos's many devices and creations—including the labyrinth and his subsequent human-powered flight from Crete with his son Ikaros—were well known in Classical Greek tragedy, as well as in Greek, Roman, and even modern tradition and iconography (Morris 1992; Farnoux 1993). So too were Theseus and his slaying of the Minotaur, aided by Minos's daughter Ariadne. Although ahistorical, or myth-historical, these traditions add to the allure and significance of the site. It is perhaps no coincidence that some of the earliest modern travelers to Crete were most interested in the legendary labyrinth of Daidalos.

Aesthetic value

Modern activities on the site have enhanced the aesthetic value of Knossos, which attracts most current visitors to the site. Whatever its accuracy, Evans's restoration of the palace conveys an idea of the original building, with its various complex and multifunctional architectural units.[7]

A heightened aesthetic sensibility and high-quality artisanship are evident in the original architectural design, masonry, and fittings and in many of the numerous finds, in a variety of materials, now in the Heraklion Museum. Foremost of these are the frescoes, among the earliest monumental wall and floor paintings in Europe, replicas of which were set up in various parts of the palace—though seldom in their original positions. In addition, Knossos is a pleasant place to visit, not least for the trees that Evans planted all around the palace to create a green zone. The palace site is located on a hill—in part natural, in part constructed—with views of the surrounding countryside. The aesthetic value of the site and of the greater landscape is enhanced by these symbolic and associative values.

The design and aesthetic qualities of the palace and of the many finds excavated there, such as the frescoes and the floral and marine motifs on Minoan pottery, have had an influence on the art and architecture of the early twentieth century, particularly the Art Nouveau and Art Deco movements of Europe and North America (Bammer 1990).

Social value

The site of Knossos today means many things to many people, particularly in Greece. The social value of the site is reflected in the fact that Knossos is an undeniable source of national, especially Cretan, pride. Because they are so recognizable, images of restored parts of the palace and especially of individual finds—frescoes, bronzes, pottery, and other media—have been used as emblems in a variety of modern products, ranging from souvenirs and the famed natural produce of Crete to logos of major shipping companies.

Knossos is the second-most-visited site in Greece and one of the most-visited archaeological sites in the world (Tables 1–7 present a summary of visitor traffic in Knossos and other main sites in Greece). It therefore represents an important economic resource, both on a national level, through intake at the gate, and on a local level. The effects of mass tourism trickle down to all aspects of the local economy, such as tourist agencies, hotels, taxi drivers, restaurants, and stores.

History of Excavation and Interventions

The palace site at Knossos has had a long and varied history of excavation and interventions, including restoration and conservation, which can be divided into six main phases, as discussed below.

History of the palace site before 1900

The earliest excavations at the site were by Minos Kalokairinos, who excavated for three months, beginning in December 1878 (Haussoullier 1880; Aposkitou 1979; Brown 1986; Hood 1987). His soundings exposed part of the central portion of the west wing of the palace, and his finds drew much attention at the time (Haussoullier 1880; Stillman 1880–81; Fabricius

Table 1 The most-visited sites in Greece, 1990–93. The Acropolis at Athens and Knossos hold the firm position as the two most-visited sites in Greece.

Rank	1990	1991	1992	1993
1	Acropolis, Athens	Acropolis, Athens	Acropolis, Athens	Acropolis, Athens
2	Knossos	Knossos	Knossos	Knossos
3	Delphi	Epidauros	Lindos	Lindos
4	Epidauros	Delphi	Epidauros	Epidauros
5	Mycenae	Lindos	Delphi	Mycenae

Sources: Data are largely derived from records kept by the Greek Ministry of Culture, particularly the Ephoreia of Prehistoric and Classical Antiquities at Heraklion; they are supplemented by material presented in Dr. Clairy Palyvou's studies on Knossos.

Table 2 Number of visitors to five major sites in Greece, 1990–93. These figures document a rise in the number of visitors to Lindos, on the island of Rhodes, and thus the growing popularity of sites on Greek islands as opposed to those on the mainland. The significant drop in the number of visitors in 1991 reflects the impact of the Gulf War on tourism in the region, although by and large, the tourist industries of Crete and of Greece in general do not appear to have been as adversely affected as those of other eastern Mediterranean countries.

Site	1990	1991	1992	1993
Acropolis, Athens	1,402,367	812,519	1,063,997	1,063,997
Knossos	706,306	515,615	689,055	660,516
Lindos	419,187	290,964	402,086	423,253
Epidauros	540,596	297,528	369,081	358,853
Delphi	590,736	292,033	355,900	338,500

Sources: See note to Table 1. Data are approximate; they are mainly based on ticket sales and therefore represent the minimum of visitors. Not included are visitor statistics for Sunday or public holidays, when entrance to Greek museums and archaeological sites is free of charge. On certain Sundays (especially those connected with public holidays) there are thousands of visitors to Knossos and other sites. These figures do not include school groups, students, and scholars.

Table 3 The most-frequented sites during winter months, 1994. The pattern showing the growing popularity of island sites (see Table 2) is reversed during the winter months, when boat schedules are limited. Lindos, heavily visited during the summer, does not appear, and Knossos drops to fifth place. Sites on the mainland, easily accessed by bus, maintain a steady stream of visitors during the winter.

Rank	Site	January–March 1994
1	Acropolis, Athens	102,620
2	Delphi	25,700
3	Epidauros	23,687
4	Mycenae	22,530
5	Knossos	19,777

Sources: See note to Table 2.

Table 4 The number of visitors to the Athenian Acropolis, as well as to the three most-visited prehistoric sites in Greece, 1991.

Site	Visitors
Acropolis, Athens	812,519
Knossos	515,615
Mycenae	274,262
Phaistos	107,330

Sources: See note to Table 2.

Table 5 Number of visitors to Knossos and Phaistos, the two most-visited archaeological sites on Crete, 1987–89.

Year	Knossos	Phaistos
1987	617,917	160,160
1988	675,600	169,980
1989	652,895	170,960

Sources: See note to Table 2.

Table 6 Quarterly number of visitors to Knossos and Phaistos, 1991.

Quarter (1991)	Knossos	Phaistos
January–March	11,778	4,362
April–June	169,953	33,911
July–September	285,949	51,357
October–December	76,077	17,700

Sources: See note to Table 2.

Table 7 Monthly ticket sales at Knossos, 1987–94.

	1987	1988	1989	1990	1991	1992	1993	1994
January	—	1,700	4,310	2,344	1,847	1,784	1,617	2,644
February	—	2,100	3,153	2,690	1,043	1,522	1,182	1,724
March	11,417	14,554	22,846	10,300	8,888	5,316	7,602	15,609
April	72,800	66,900	53,300	68,780	25,862	73,884	60,925	67,314
May	83,900	84,300	87,700	89,400	59,262	94,048	76,921	94,087
June	81,100	86,300	77,700	89,200	84,829	86,613	79,156	91,899
July	109,200	105,300	92,700	105,947	116,492	106,500	102,952	112,196
August	88,400	128,200	111,700	132,598	84,829	122,699	124,668	129,517
September	86,800	96,400	101,900	110,851	84,628	108,994	106,355	110,089
October	74,300	75,600	83,800	77,701	67,746	79,675	35,696	53,407
November	8,000	9,950	9,700	12,863	6,827	5,643	10,654	10,459
December	2,200	4,040	4,186	3,630	1,503	2,377	2,788	2,612
Total	618,117	675,344	652,995	706,304	543,756	689,055	610,516	691,557

Sources: See note to Table 2. (Figures prior to March 1987 are not available.)

1886; Evans 1894). Kalokairinos chanced upon several inscribed symbols on gypsum blocks, now referred to as "masons' marks"; it was these marks, perhaps more than anything else, that drew Evans to the site.[8] He first visited the site in 1894, quickly purchased the land, and set about planning its excavation; for a variety of political and economic reasons, however, he was not able to begin until 1900 (Evans 1899–1900:4–5; Hood and Taylor 1981:1–2).

Excavations and activities of Arthur Evans, phase 1 (circa 1900–1913)

Apart from a nine-year gap bridging the First World War, and several shorter periods of hiatus, Evans excavated the site from 1900 to 1930. From the point of view of restoration and conservation, his activities may be divided into two broad phases separated by the war. The first phase saw the full-scale excavation of the site. The main part of the palace was uncovered during the first six seasons, from 1900 to 1905 (Fig. 4), and the results were promptly presented in detailed annual preliminary reports (Evans 1899–1900, 1900–1901, 1901–2, 1902–3, 1903–4, 1904–5).

By modern standards the excavations left a lot to be desired, particularly the pace with which the work was conducted and the fact that a great deal of archaeological material, especially pottery, was discarded. Nevertheless—because Evans from the beginning worked closely with a capable team of specialists—the excavations were remarkably ahead of their time.[9] A large observation tower, which also served for photography, was soon built by the excavators at the southeast edge of the Central Court (Brown 1983:18, fig. 3; Evans 1900–1901:96–97, pl. 2). This allowed for a level of photography rarely seen in contemporary archaeology. The meticulous photographic record kept by the excavators, now housed in the Evans Archive at the Ashmolean Museum, Oxford, included an aerial view of the palace that was published in 1935 (Evans 1935:pt. 1, xxvi–xxvii).

Although this first phase of Evans's work at the site was largely devoted to excavation, the conservation of various parts of the palace became a pressing problem from the very beginning. This was particularly the case for two of the most prominent sectors of the palace, the so-called Throne Room (Figs. 5–12) and the Residential, or Domestic, Quarter surrounding the Grand Staircase (Figs. 13–20).[10] By 1927 Evans stated, "Knossos, as was remarked by a German colleague, has passed through three 'periods' of conservation—marked respectively by the use of wooden supports, of iron girders, and of ferro-concrete" (Evans 1927:262). The first phase of Evans's intervention is that of wooden supports and iron girders.

One of the earliest and most spectacular discoveries of the first season, the Throne Room presented problems of conservation from the start (Figs. 5, 6). When a gypsum floor, benches, and fresco fragments

Figure 5

Throne Room during excavation, 1900. This photograph, touched up with white ink, was published as the main illustration of the appeal brochure issued by the Cretan Exploration Fund in 1900 (see Brown 1983:36, pl. 14). Note the poor state of preservation at the time of excavation.

Figure 6

Throne Room viewed from the east in 1900, after the first year of excavation. The discovery in situ of parts of the gypsum floor and wall frescoes made it evident that some form of immediate protection from the elements was necessary. Evans stands in front of the tent in the background.

were discovered, it was clear that some sort of protective cover for the Throne Room was urgently needed. The first roofing solution was completed in 1901. It consisted of a flat roof supported by brick pillars along the sides. Columns—constructed of wooden slats, covered with plaster, and painted—were fitted into positions formerly occupied by Minoan columns, where they supported a timber framework. The structure was further protected by wrought iron railings and iron gates (Fig. 7). In 1904 the flat roof was replaced by a more permanent structure with a pitched roof supported by metal girders (Fig. 8). The loft of the building was fitted with shelving and used as "a kind of reference museum" (Brown 1983:42); it saw service for quite a number of years before being replaced in 1930 by a massive structure of reinforced concrete, which attempted to convey an idea of the original (Figs. 9, 12). Although providing a solution for the Throne Room, the various structures of this phase protected only a small

Figure 7

First protective roof over the Throne Room, viewed from the southeast, 1901. The flat roof was supported by brick pillars along the sides and by interior columns that were made of wooden slats, covered with plaster, and painted. The interior columns, which supported a timber framework, were fitted into positions occupied by the original Minoan columns. For protection, the enclosure was fitted with wrought iron railings and iron gates. The protective structure covered only the Throne Room; most of the extensive excavation was exposed to the elements.

Figure 8

Second roof over the Throne Room, viewed from the southeast, 1904. The earlier flat roof (Fig. 7) was replaced by a more permanent structure with a pitched roof supported by metal girders. The loft was fitted with shelving and served as a reference museum.

Figure 9

Throne Room viewed from the southeast, 1930. The functional second shelter for the Throne Room (Fig. 8) was replaced by a massive structure of reinforced concrete based on Evans's idea of the original Minoan building. This included the construction of the entirely modern upper story, used as a "picture gallery" for copies of frescoes from various parts of the palace. The newly restored Stepped Portico, Throne Room complex, and West Portico of the North Entrance Passage can be seen.

Figure 10

Throne Room, Anteroom, and Stepped Portico after excavation, 1900. The fragility of the original fabric of the monument can be seen in the prerestoration state of the Throne Room and its immediate surrounds.

Figure 11

Interior of the Throne Room as restored in 1930. Three copies of the Griffin Fresco were added to the original, fragmentary griffin discovered in situ in 1900. The restoration is dramatic in the degree to which it transformed the excavated remains of the area (Figs. 5, 6) (see color plate 2c).

Figure 12
Throne Room complex and the Stepped Portico, viewed from the east after restoration, 1930. There is a substantial difference between the excavated remains (Fig. 10) and the result of the restoration. The new concrete structure was laid directly onto the original fabric.

portion of the excavated area, and substantial areas on the west side of the palace, including the West Magazines, were left exposed (Brown 1983:pls. 32, 33a–c).

Other conservation and consolidation work conducted during the early years included the construction of a large retaining wall, built on the east side of the Central Court by 1902 (Fig. 4). In 1903 the Theatral Area was consolidated and restored with a retaining wall on the north side (Fig. 21), and in 1904 a stone shelter was erected over the Magazines of the Giant Pithoi (Hood and Taylor 1981:4).

The excavation of the Grand Staircase and the Domestic Quarter, with evidence of upper floors preserved in places, presented formidable problems (Hood and Taylor 1981:2–5; Brown 1983:77–84). Photographs of the area taken in the course of excavations show the poorly preserved and friable nature of many of the exposed remains (Figs. 13, 14). Stairs and floors that had partially caved in, along with collapsed windows and doorways originally supported in antiquity by wooden beams, necessitated immediate attention and support. The first solution was to prop up fallen architectural members with wooden supports (Fig. 14), and by the end of 1902, much had been done on the consolidation of this area of the palace

Figure 13
Area of the Grand Staircase during excavation, 1901. The poorly preserved and friable nature of many of the exposed remains of the Domestic Quarter can be seen. This unique and important part of the site required immediate attention. Evans found significant evidence of upper floors: stairs and floors that had partially caved in, as well as collapsed windows and doorways supported in antiquity by wooden beams.

Figure 14, above
Domestic Quarter viewed from the east, 1901.
From left to right are the Hall of the Double
Axes, part of the stairs leading to the upper
East-West Corridor, and the Lobby of the
Wooden Posts. The first solution to the prob-
lem of collapsed floors, stairs, windows, and
doors was the use of wooden supports to
prop up fallen architectural members. This
area was restored in 1928 (see Fig. 18).

(Figs. 15, 16). Further major work of restoration was undertaken in this
area in 1905, as well as in 1908 and 1910 (Fig. 17). Part of this work consisted of replacing or repositioning landing blocks and other fallen architectural elements, while part required the replacing of earlier wooden
supports with iron girders (Fig. 17). A number of stone columns (plastered
over, painted, and fitted into original sockets) had replaced the earlier
wooden supports.[11] Moreover, a good deal of rebuilding in stone had been
undertaken, with the additional support of iron girders set in cement in

Figure 15
Area of the Grand Staircase, 1902–5. This bird's-eye view from the west,
taken from the observation tower, shows the wooden supports that have
been put into place in the East-West Corridor, as well as the lower
flights of stairs. In this early stage of the work, attention was given to
stabilization and consolidation, largely achieved with wooden supports.

Figure 16
Area of the Grand Staircase, the Hall of the Double Axes, and the
Queen's Megaron, 1902. Wooden supports were used for stabilization
and consolidation.

Figure 17
Grand Staircase during restoration, 1910. The wooden supports initially used to stabilize the structures (see Figs. 15, 16) were replaced a few years later by iron girders. Arthur Evans, dressed in white, is seen at the upper center right; next to him stand Duncan Mackenzie (wearing a pith helmet), Evans's assistant and supervising field archaeologist, and the architect Christian Doll (wearing the wide-brimmed hat).

Figure 18
Lobby of the Wooden Posts after restoration, viewed from the east, 1928. The period between 1922 and 1930 saw the most radical reconstruction work. During this time the site was transformed from poorly preserved ruins (Fig. 14) into a multistoried concrete vision of the past.

the place of the original architraves and beams. Despite these developments, however, the reinforced concrete roofing over parts of the area—especially the larger halls—was not realized until after 1922.

It was also during this phase that Evans planted trees all around the site, in order to set off the palace from the surrounding landscape. The trees began to appear in photographs of the site taken after 1904.

In a number of publications, Evans stressed the need to address the problems of conservation at the site (Evans 1927, 1935:1–18). An exceptionally wet winter in 1904 led to the collapse of part of the Grand

Staircase; this event, in turn, threatened much of the Domestic Quarter, and Evans felt that "to avert the ruin thus threatened demanded nothing less than heroic measures" (Evans 1904–5:23). Although in this first phase of activity, Evans was basically concerned with consolidation, the extremely perishable nature of the excavated materials led him to believe that more invasive interventions were required.[12] At the time this position was strongly supported by many of his contemporaries (Karo 1959:16–27), although his interventions of 1922 to 1930 (described below) were to later become very controversial.

Activities of Arthur Evans, phase 2 (1922–1930)

This was the period of the most radical reconstruction, during which the site was transformed from poorly preserved ruins into a multistoried concrete vision of the past. In comparison to the first phase, the resumption of activities in 1922, after the First World War, saw a series of smaller soundings, whereas the restoration of the palace continued with increased momentum (Hood and Taylor 1981:3–4).[13] Evans aimed to provide the visitor with an impression of how parts of the palace might have looked in their heyday, sometime in the early part of the late Minoan period. He set forth his reasons for the restoration, which he referred to as *reconstitution,* in a paper read before the Society of Antiquaries of London (Evans 1927). His reconstruction aroused much controversy at the time, and it has continued to do so ever since.[14]

While the use of wood and iron characterized the reconstruction work of the first phase, during this second phase, ferroconcrete was used extensively, with serious consequences. In his 1927 paper Evans stated, "The new facilities afforded by the use of reinforced concrete made it possible not only to renew in a more substantial form the supports of upper elements in the west section of the palace, but to profit by a better understanding of the meaning of existing remains" (Evans 1927:264). In 1922 and 1923, portions of the upper floor over the West Wing and the staircase associated with the Stepped Portico were restored (Brown 1983:pls. 25, 27a). Further reconstruction was undertaken in 1925 at various points of the palace at the south and southwest sides of the Central Court (Hood and Taylor 1981:5).

The west side of the South Propylaeum was restored in 1926, where a replica of the Cupbearer Fresco was installed. Most of the work of restoration on the Grand Staircase and the Domestic Quarter was undertaken in 1928. The Loggia of the Grand Staircase was restored and roofed over, and a replica of the Shield Fresco was executed (Brown 1983:pl. 56c); a replica of the Dolphin Fresco was set up in the Queen's Megaron. In the same year the whole Hall of the Double Axes, including the porticoes, was roofed over with reinforced concrete, and the upper floor was relaid at its original height (Brown 1983:83) (Figs. 19, 20). In 1929 the Southwest Columnar Chamber was erected above the Southwest Pillar Crypt, several of the West Magazines were roofed over, and the North Lustral Basin was restored (Fig. 22) (Hood and Taylor 1981:5).[15]

Figure 19
Restored upper story of the Domestic
Quarter, 1928. This bird's-eye view from the
west, taken from the observation tower,
shows that the restorations extended to the
second stories of some structures. This photograph can be compared to Figure 16, which
shows the area after partial restoration but
before the 1928 erection of the second story.
The roof over the lower story was built of
reinforced concrete.

Figure 20
South colonnade of the restored Hall of the
Double Axes, viewed from the south after the
work of 1928. The entirely modern columns
are based on images from Minoan frescoes.
During the work of the 1920s, some parts of
the palace were restored on the basis of fragmentary, and often little-understood, Minoan
iconography.

Figure 21
Theatral Area after consolidation and restoration, viewed from the northwest, 1930. One
of the areas worked on during the first phase
of intervention, the Theatral Area was consolidated and partially reconstructed. The north
supporting wall was rebuilt; missing slabs of
the northeast section of the southern flight of
steps were restored; and a number of sunken
slabs were partially raised. The restored parts
are indicated in an early published plan (Evans
1902–3:103, fig. 68).

Figure 22
North Lustral Basin viewed from the north-west, as restored in 1929. Parts of the palace were restored according to the architectural fashion of the day. Consequently, they are considered by some to be the best-preserved and finest examples of Art Deco and Art Nouveau architecture in Greece.

The work of reconstruction was brought to a climax in 1930 with the completion of the Throne Room and the North Portico overlooking the North Entrance Passage. The Throne Room was roofed over for a third time to achieve its present form (Figs. 9, 11, 12); this included the construction, in reinforced concrete, of the entirely modern upper story, used as a picture gallery for copies of frescoes from various parts of the palace (Brown 1983:42). In the Throne Room itself, three additional copies of the Griffin Fresco were added to the earlier griffin, restored in 1913 by Edouard Gilliéron (Fig. 11). Providing one of the main entrances to the palace, the North Entrance Passage, largely cleared in 1900–1901, was restored and rebuilt in 1930, complete with a restored replica of the Charging Bull Fresco set up in the portico built on top of the restored west bastion (Figs. 23, 24). The west facade of the palace was also radically transformed in the restorations of 1930 (Figs. 25, 26).

Figure 23
Portion of the North Entrance Passage as first exposed after excavation, viewed from the north-northeast, 1901. The later reconstruction of these excavated remains was to rely heavily on conjecture (Fig. 24).

Figure 24
Portico of the North Entrance Passage, viewed from the north-northeast, 1930. As part of the reconstruction of the excavated remains (Fig. 23), a copy of the Charging Bull Fresco was installed in the portico.

Figure 25
West Court and west facade of the palace, viewed from the south-southwest after 1904 and before 1930. The original foundation of the wall of the west facade of the palace is seen sometime before the completion of restoration in 1930 (Fig. 26). Perhaps more so than for any other archaeological monument in the Mediterranean, the restoration of the palace (as distinct from the preserved remains of the original building seen here) has developed its own historical identity.

Figure 26
West Court and west facade of the palace, viewed from the southwest after 1930. The reconstructed wall of the palace was built in concrete directly on the original fabric (Fig. 25). The weight of the new materials on the deteriorated archaeological remains has exacerbated their process of decay.

Aftermath of the Second World War

Immediately after the Second World War, Nikolaos Platon and R. W. Hutchinson conducted an initial campaign of cleaning and conservation; Platon also undertook a major campaign of repairs in the palace between 1955 and 1960 (Hood and Taylor 1981:5; with brief annual accounts in *Kretika Chronika*). After the war, various parts of the palace were roofed over. The area above the Royal Magazines on the east side, for example, as well as part of the upper floor built by Evans over the West Wing, was roofed in concrete (Hood and Taylor 1981:5).[16]

During this period, the problem of the future responsibility for the site, including its maintenance, was addressed. In 1926, at the age of seventy-five, Evans transferred all his personal rights—in the palace; in his personal house on the site, called the Villa Ariadne; and in the Knossos estate—to the British School of Archaeology at Athens, with the necessary assent of the Greek government.[17] To supplement income derived from the estate (wine, olives, oil, and grain), Evans established securities toward the maintenance of the site and created an endowment for a curator. It was hoped that the arrangements of 1926 would provide for all emergencies, since the total endowment was estimated to yield £350 a year, and until 1941 the endowment was supplemented by the income from the estate. During the Second World War, however, the estate fell out of cultivation, and the increasing costs in the period immediately after the war made it impossible for the British School to maintain its activities at Knossos. In 1951 the Managing Committee of the school proposed to the Greek government, through the British Embassy in Athens and with the concurrence of the British Foreign Office, to hand over the palace with the villa and the freehold estate held in trust for its maintenance. The offer was accepted by the Greek government on the centenary of Evans's birth;[18] since 1951 the Greek Archaeological Service has been entirely responsible for the conservation and maintenance of Knossos.

The problem of the maintenance of the site, particularly in light of the growing number of visitors, was deemed serious enough to warrant mention in a 1951 article in the *Times* of London that states: "There is also the problem of future maintenance. Growing suburbs of Herakleion (formerly Candia) are already within walking distance; a vast sanatorium will soon break the skyline; while restaurants, cafés, and shacks, with nocturnal radio, occupy adjacent freeholds which the school cannot afford to buy out. At week-ends and festivals, which are frequent in Crete, the palace is thronged by hundreds of local visitors, many of whom regard it rather as a recreation ground than an ancient site, and need supervision if damage is to be avoided" (Myres 1951:7).

Recent excavations

Much supplementary archaeological work has been carried out on the immediate palace site. Most of it has focused on closer study and reinterpretation of materials excavated by Evans, including closer scrutiny of the photographs, plans, drawings, notebooks, and labels of the early excavators.[19] More recent excavations have concentrated on the Minoan town, as well as on the pre- and post-Minoan areas in and around the palace.

Although excavations in the area of the site beyond the palace were initiated in 1900 by D. G. Hogarth (Hogarth 1899–1900), and much work—in terms of both excavation and restoration—was conducted by Evans himself (Evans 1911–14), the great extent of the site assured future researchers of new discoveries. Many of these were made in the years following the Second World War, and they continue to be made.[20] Recent excavations have pushed back the prehistory of the site to an even more remote past, in addition to clarifying much of the history of the site in the pre-Palatial Bronze Age. The Neolithic settlement of Knossos, mostly located below the palace itself and first uncovered by Evans, was excavated more thoroughly by J. D. Evans between 1957 and 1970 (Evans 1964, 1971, 1994; Warren et al. 1968; Furness 1953). During these excavations, large areas of the Central Court, as well as smaller parts of the West Court and elsewhere, were investigated (Hood and Smyth 1981:6). Early Iron Age, Greek, Hellenistic, Roman, and early Byzantine Knossos prior to the Arab invasion have received much attention in the years since Arthur Evans, and numerous excavations have been conducted in the area beyond the palace (Brock 1957; Coldstream 1973; Sackett et al. 1992; Hood and Smyth 1981:16–27; Myers, Myers, and Cadogan 1992:145–46).

Recent conservation, maintenance problems, and future plans

The most recent conservation and maintenance efforts at Knossos have focused on repairs to Evans's reconstruction and on visitor management.

The extensive use of reinforced concrete earlier in this century, the process of natural weathering, and the incidence of mass tourism have combined to create a difficult conservation challenge—not only for the fabric of the original monument but also for that of Evans's restoration. In certain parts of the reconstructed palace, the concrete poured almost seventy years ago has decayed, exposing many of the reinforcing iron girders, which have themselves begun to decay, thereby threatening the entire structure (Fig. 27). In other parts of the palace, reinforced concrete was used in places where it proved to be structurally unsound.[21] Moreover, because he often poured concrete directly onto original remains, Evans's interventions are largely irreversible. This practice has necessitated recent repair, consolidation, and additional support, not only to the original fabric but also to Evans's restorations.

A second source of problems is the arrival of mass tourism on the site. The onslaught, especially during the summer months, of large groups of visitors, many of which arrive at the same time because of their tour schedules, has placed great pressure on both the original fabric of the monument and on the structural integrity of the restoration. Expanses of original paving, for example, have been much eroded, both by natural weathering and by foot traffic; in many formerly paved areas, all that survives is the concrete setting poured by Evans around original flagstones (Fig. 28).

Many other parts of Evans's restoration have also been adversely affected by direct human contact (Fig. 29). Sections of the palace have been closed to public access for some time for repair, and a visitor management plan is needed. Almost fifteen years ago the Greek government declared its intent to proceed with such a plan, and in 1993, the study subsequently commissioned was carried out by Dr. Clairy Palyvou. Although funding for

Figure 27
Detail of exposed and decaying iron supports in the roof of the Domestic Quarter, 1994. The extensive use of reinforced concrete earlier in this century, the natural process of weathering, and mass tourism have combined to create a difficult conservation challenge, not only for the fabric of the original monument but also for that of Arthur Evans's restoration.

Figure 28

East-West Corridor of the Domestic Quarter, viewed from the west, 1994. While the original paving slabs have been largely eroded by natural weathering as well as foot traffic, the concrete poured in 1928 is often much better preserved. Damage and wear, the effects of which are seen here, have prompted the recent conservation of both the original fabric of the palace and that of Evans's restoration; moreover, these concerns necessitated a visitor management plan.

Figure 29

Visitors in the Central Court, viewed from the northwest, 1994. Largely the product of a single man's vision and interpretation, the palace is one of the best-known and most-visited archaeological sites in Greece and the Mediterranean (see Tables 1–7). Because of similar tour schedules, large groups of visitors arrive during the summer months at the same time; their onset has placed great pressure both on the original fabric of the monument and on the structural integrity of the restoration.

its implementation was approved by vote in 1995, the plan has not yet gone into effect.[22] Future plans for the palace have also been strongly influenced by a growing literature on various technical advances—such as an improved understanding of the physical properties of the original fabric, as well as seismic hazard assessments (see, among other recent studies, Papageorgakis and Mposkos 1988; Makropoulos, Drakopoulos, and Tselentis 1988; Brachert 1991; Moraiti and Christaras 1992).

Issues Addressed

An archaeological site like Knossos has many values, some of which have already been mentioned. When decisions are made about a site, attempts to uphold all the values can create immediate conflicts; problems can also arise later when certain values are given preeminence over others. In the case of Knossos, many of the key issues that require attention stem from the reconstruction and restoration carried out by Sir Arthur Evans. The restoration, one of the largest and earliest of its kind, has placed the historical and scientific values in conflict with some of the social and economic values. The need to balance the historical values of a site and its surroundings with the demands of mass tourism is an issue common to many archaeological sites in the Mediterranean. At the same time, the example of Knossos emphasizes certain issues more clearly than others. Among these, the following may be singled out for discussion.

Prominence given to one historic phase

Evans's restoration, although in part representing an amalgam of various Minoan phases, disregards significant earlier and later remains at the site. The casual visitor—and often even the specialist—can forget that Knossos is the largest Neolithic site on Crete (the excavated Neolithic remains are largely reburied under the Central and West Courts of the later palace) and, along with Gortyna, is one of the two largest Greek and Roman sites on the island. During the early Iron Age (1100–600 B.C.E.), Knossos may have been a large and thriving urban nucleus (Coldstream 1991). Evans's restoration not only neglects the historical significance of the site during other periods but, in fact, actively hides their remains. Similarly, of the numerous monuments excavated within the vicinity of the palace, the ones that have been restored are mostly of the Minoan period.

Extent and accuracy of the restoration

The scale and extent of Evans's reconstruction and restoration have posed a number of problems for the subsequent study of the original remains. In certain parts of the monument, it is difficult to distinguish original architectural elements from restored ones, and in other parts it is often difficult to establish whether original elements incorporated in the reconstruction are in their original positions or have instead been moved from elsewhere. Indeed, the impact of these problems on future research on the original remains was a concern expressed as early as 1927 by the president of the Society of Antiquaries of London.[23]

The question of the accuracy of the restoration in light of current research and knowledge has received much attention. Because of the meticulous photographic records kept by the excavators, and especially of the detailed notebooks of daily activities maintained by Duncan Mackenzie, Evans's assistant and supervising field archaeologist, it is possible to reconstruct, to a certain extent, some of the elements of Evans's restoration. It is clear, for example, that some details of the restoration are wrong—the position of certain frescoes, even the number of floors in parts of the monument.[24] Moreover, some parts of the palace were restored on the basis of fragmentary, and perhaps little-understood, Minoan iconography, whereas others were restored in the light of the architectural fashion of the day. This is most noticeable in the area of and around the Throne Room, parts of which closely resemble Art Nouveau and Art Deco buildings of the 1920s (see especially Figs. 12, 22). Furthermore, although Evans's expressed aim was to preserve the record of the upper floors of the building revealed by the process of excavation (Evans 1927:258), the use that some of the restored upper stories were put to was not always commensurate with Minoan practice. A good example is the "picture gallery" above the Throne Room, an entirely modern upper story used for the display of replicas of frescoes from various parts of the palace.

Introduction of modern building materials

Related to the issue of accuracy, but itself a source of further problems, is the heavy reliance on reinforced concrete, a material alien to the original building. Regarded by Evans as a virtual panacea, reinforced concrete permitted more substantial solutions than wood or iron girders could afford.[25] Quite apart from the issue of the compatibility of reinforced concrete with the original fabric of the monument is the whole question of reconstruction in permanent or semipermanent materials that do not permit reversibility.

Historical identity of Evans's restoration

Perhaps more so than for any other archaeological monument in the Mediterranean, the *restoration* of the palace at Knossos—as distinct from the original building—has developed its own historical identity. Largely the result of one man's vision and interpretation, the palace is one of the best-known and most-visited archaeological sites in Greece and the Mediterranean (Tables 1–7). Evans's restoration has itself assumed historical significance; this is nowhere more obvious than in the most recent conservation at the site, which has focused on repairing and consolidating the reinforced concrete poured by Evans. There has even been reluctance to cut down any of the trees planted by Evans, even ones that have interfered with recent excavations or that threaten various parts of the palace.

Long-term maintenance of the site

The example of Knossos raises the question of responsibility for long-term conservation and maintenance—an issue common to many Mediterranean archaeological sites where excavations have been conducted by members of foreign schools or institutions. The excavations at Knossos constitute one of the most visible, long-term projects undertaken by a foreign school in Greece. Following Evans, several generations of British scholars worked on the palace itself, as well as on many other buildings and cemeteries of various periods at the site. Although the scholarly work on Knossos, including a long list of prestigious publications, has been mainly carried out by members of a foreign school, the direct responsibility for conservation and maintenance has fallen since 1951 on the shoulders of a national authority, the Greek Archaeological Service. This history raises the issue of the role currently played, or to be played, by foreign institutions in the protection of the cultural resources of a host nation.

Acknowledgments

This study would not have been possible without the support and cooperation of the Greek Ministry of Culture and, particularly, of the director of antiquities, Dr. Yiannis Tsedakis, and his staff. Among others, Dr. Jordan Dimakopoulos discussed various aspects of the project during its early stages and provided much useful advice. From the very outset, the generous and unstinting support of the Heraklion Ephoreia assured its success. Special thanks are due to the ephor for prehistoric and classical antiquities at Heraklion, Dr. Alexandra Karetsou. She gave freely of her time and energy and placed at the author's disposal all the various records and other information pertaining to Knossos and its surrounds (especially the information provided in Tables 5–7), as well as providing access to all parts of the archaeological site. Thanks are also due to the members of her staff, particularly Dr. Georgios Rethemiotakis. Various members of the British School of Archaeology at Athens have contributed greatly to the project. In this respect, thanks are due to the successive directors of the school, Dr. Elizabeth French and the late Dr. Martin Price, and especially to Dr. Colin Macdonald, the Knossos curator. Together Dr. Macdonald and Dr. Rethemiotakis were instrumental in facilitating the conference site visit. The extensive archives of Sir Arthur Evans, including the excavation daybooks and the original photographs, now held in the Ashmolean Museum, Oxford, were placed at the author's disposal by the keeper of antiquities, Dr. P. R. S. Moorey; thanks are owed to him, as well as to Dr. Andrew Sherratt and Dr. Michael Vickers, senior assistant keepers. From the very outset of this project, the author has benefited greatly from numerous discussions with Dr. Clairy Palyvou, to whom he is most grateful. He has drawn heavily on both her encyclopedic knowledge of Minoan architecture and, particularly, her detailed knowledge of Knossos. Finally, the author wishes to thank his colleagues Dr. Martha Demas and Dr. Nicholas Stanley-Price for the pleasure of their company, as well as for initiating a novice into the mysteries of site management.

Notes

1. Thus the title of Evans's four-volume account of his excavations at Knossos (Evans 1921, 1928, 1930, 1935). The building on the Kephala Hill was interpreted as a palace soon after the original excavations by Minos Kalokairinos; thus Heinrich Schliemann, Wilhelm Dörpfeld, and Ernst Fabricius thought that the remains uncovered by Kalokairinos belonged to a Mycenaean palace (Evans 1899–1900:4; cf. Haussoullier 1880; Fabricius 1886). The American W. J. Stillman believed the remains to be the legendary labyrinth (Stillman 1880–81). For the contemporary excavations in the town and cemeteries, see Hogarth (1899–1900).

2. The site is located at 35°18′ north, 25°10′ east. See further Myers, Myers, and Cadogan (1992:134–36), including a brief summary of the geomorphology of the area. The physical environment of the Knossos area is also overviewed by Roberts in Hood and Smyth (1981:5); see also Hood and Taylor (1981:1).

3. The area stretches from the road bridge over the streambed north of Ayios Ioannis in the north to Spilia in the south, and from the summit of Ailias (Ayios Elias) on the east to Fortetsa in the west (Hood and Smyth 1981).

4. These are clearly marked on the map (Hood and Smyth 1981) and include the modern village of Knossos (formerly Bougada Metochi) west of the palace; Makryteichos on the west bank of the Kairatos, northeast of the palace; Fortetsa, Ambelokipi (Teke) and Ayios Ioannis to the west and north; and Kallithéa (Babali) to the northeast.

5. As early as 1927 Arthur Evans could claim, "Although in the work of conservation and reconstitution of the upper stories new lines have been recently struck out at Pompeii, at Ostia, and elsewhere, it may be fairly said that they have followed the example already set on the site of Knossos, where the work has now proceeded with successively improving methods for twenty-six years" (Evans 1927:258).

6. Much of this is related by the Athenian historian Thucydides (1.4), writing in the fifth century B.C.E.

7. The reaction of most modern visitors—including those of the conference—to Evans's interventions is sympathetic, if not favorable. See the comments in Stanley-Price and Sullivan (1995).

8. Evans was particularly interested in an early form of Aegean writing, predating alphabetic Greek; see Evans (1894:270–372; 1899–1900). He writes, "The curious signs on the gypsum blocks seemed to have a bearing on the special object of my investigations, the existence, namely, in Crete of a prehistoric system of writing" (Evans 1899–1900:4). Evans's expectations were rewarded with the discovery of Linear B tablets from the first season of excavations. See also Evans (1908, 1909).

9. Among the specialists was Duncan Mackenzie (Fig. 17), Evans's assistant and the supervising field archaeologist responsible for much of the excavation documentation; he was recently described as one of the first scientific workers in the Aegean (Brown 1983:19; Momigliano 1995). As architects, Evans also employed Theodore Fyfe (1900–1904) and later Christian Doll (1905–10) (Fig. 17). It was Fyfe who drew the first general plan of the site (published in Evans 1899–1900:pls. 12, 13); he later went on to become the director of the Cambridge School of Architecture (1922–36) and was the first to publish a paper fully devoted to the conservation and restoration of the palace (Fyfe 1926). C. C. T. Doll, then architectural student of the British School at Athens, was responsible for the massive task of restoring the Grand Staircase of the Domestic Quarter (see Evans 1904–5:23–26; 1927). Evans was also able to afford the services of the Swiss artist Emile Gilliéron—who first visited the site as early as 1900—and later of his son Edouard, who were both responsible for restoring the frescoes. The elder Gilliéron served as professor of drawing to the royal Greek court; he also ran a business in Athens making copies of ancient works of art. Even the first foreman of the excavation, Gregorios Antoniou, brought from Cyprus, was an experienced excavator, having spent his youth robbing tombs in Cyprus; in later years he assisted D. G. Hogarth on excavations in Cyprus and Crete (Brown 1983:15).

10. See Hood and Taylor (1981:5). The names used by Evans for the various parts of the palace are often hypothetical, even fanciful; although they can sometimes be bewildering, they have been in constant use by scholars throughout this century and thus have entered into common archaeological usage (Hood and Taylor 1981:7). For this reason, they are considered to be proper names, rather than descriptive references to the site.

11. The wooden columns were modeled after those depicted in various fresco fragments discovered in 1904. Many of the iron girders, imported to Crete at great expense, had fallen into the harbor during their unloading at Heraklion (Brown 1983:81).

12. See Shaw (1971). The fragility of the remains is vividly described by the Italian anthropologist Angelo Mosso. In 1907 he wrote, with reference to the Minoan palace of Phaistos, excavated by the Scuola Archeologica di Atene e delle Missioni Italiane in Oriente:

    The alabaster, from its exposure to the weather, has lost the ivory polish and transparency, and has now the grey shade of melted silver. The water which has flowed over it has dried up the azure and roseate veins which had had the effect of

arabesques upon a pearl-coloured ground. I grieved to think that I was probably
the last to contemplate the rose-tinted squares of this fine pavement, and I felt both
sad and uneasy as I walked upon the slabs, which creaked and splintered as if it
were a thin layer of ice upon the marble. Some of the blocks are black as velvet
from the action of fire, while others are pure white, and have become like sponge
beneath the corroding rain, giving the effect of snow on ice or of hailstones
heaped up in a ditch after a storm.

   Within a century the palaces of Phæstos will exist no longer, and the ruins
will only be seen in books. These witnesses of primæval civilisation are inevitably
condemned to disappear; everything even to the last vestige will crumble to dust
and be dispersed by the wind, or will be dissolved into mud, which the rivulets of
rain will carry far off to trouble the waters of the river.

   In a few years' time nothing will remain but a limestone skeleton; the
alabaster stairs will be destroyed, the decoration of the pavements and the incrusta-
tion of the walls will have vanished.

   In perplexity we watch the ruin of the ruins. The clouds and the sun will
devour the sacred relics of that civilisation which was the mother of our own. The
vision of these remains brought back to the light has been like a flower which has
bloomed unexpectedly to show us the beauty and perfume of pre-Hellenic art—it
will disappear sadly, inevitably, but its fragrance, its fruitful germs will last beyond
the limits of time. (Mosso 1907:66–68)

13.   Although Mackenzie still served as Evans's assistant, much of the work of reconstruction
      was supervised at this time by the architect-draftsman Piet de Jong. Appointed in 1922,
      de Jong went on to serve as Knossos curator (1947–52) and was involved with the site until
      his death in 1967 (Brown 1983:30).

14.   For contemporary criticisms of Evans's work, see the published discussion in Evans
      (1927:266–67); see also Picard (1932:3–18, 49–60, 105–16) and Graham (1962, especially p. 26).
      For a more recent view, see Bintliff (1984). It is interesting to contrast the view of the youth-
      ful Hazel ffennell (her spelling), who visited the site in 1922 (prior to the extensive use of
      reinforced concrete) and was greatly unimpressed by the ruins; her thoughts on the site are
      quoted in Brown (1983:58).

15.   It was also during this phase, on the evening of 26 June 1926, that a severe earthquake struck
      the area, at a time when Evans and his team were at Knossos. The site itself, including the
      restorations completed up to that time, was not adversely affected. The same was not true,
      however, for the Archaeological Museum of Heraklion, which housed the more important
      finds from Knossos and numerous other sites in Crete. The most telling photographs of the
      damage caused to the museum and to individual objects within it were published in the
      newspaper the *Sphere* (1926:137).

16.   It should be noted that since 1955, all roofing has been constructed of lightweight translu-
      cent material supported on thin steel poles.

17.   Evans built the Villa Ariadne for himself near the site in 1906–7 (its construction was super-
      vised by Christian Doll, and it incorporated many of the same architectural details used in
      the reconstruction of the palace) (Brown 1983:30; Powell 1973). In 1931 Evans returned to
      Crete and, with John Pendlebury and Piet de Jong, excavated the Temple Tomb. His final
      visit to the site was in 1935, when he was honored with a ceremony and the unveiling of the
      bronze bust dedicated to him; the bust still stands in the West Court. He died six years later,
      at the age of ninety, at his home on Boars Hill at Oxford.

18.   A useful account of these transactions was published in an article written by Professor Sir
      John Myres (1951:7). Among other things, Myres states, "The visitors' fees imposed by the
      Greek Government went to the Department of Antiquities, not to the school." Myres
      appears to imply that the British School may have been able to maintain the site if it had had
      access to the income from visitors' fees.

19.   See, among many other studies, the following monographs: Popham (1964, 1970); Palmer
      and Boardman (who present opposing views) (1963); Palmer (1969); Raison (1969, 1988);
      Hallager (1977); Niemeier (1985); and Driessen (1990). Numerous articles on the subject are
      listed in Myers, Myers, and Cadogan (1992:141–42).

20. For a recent bibliography see Myers, Myers, and Cadogan (1992:142–43). For a complete survey of the Knossos area in the Bronze Age, see Hood and Smyth (1981:6–15); see also various papers in Evely, Hughes-Brock, and Momigliano (1994). For the excavation of the "Unexplored Mansion," see Popham et al. (1984).

21. For example, reinforced concrete was used in the restorations to represent woodwork, as well as other materials (Fyfe 1926:479). The fact that concrete was used to reproduce or replace wood, even in those parts where the original woodwork served a structural function that concrete could not duplicate, has resulted in problems unforeseen by Evans and his collaborators. These problems stem from the fact that concrete does not behave like wood or like other materials used in the original construction. The recent repairs to the South House at Knossos under the supervision of the Heraklion Ephoreia of Antiquities are a case in point; those repairs have largely focused on consolidating and supporting Evans's restorations.

22. The plan prepared by Dr. Palyvou, which in part entailed designing a route (or routes) for visitors to the site of the palace of Knossos, essentially aimed to provide special passageways, ramps, and wooden stairs in order to minimize the direct contact of visitors both with the original fabric of the monument and with Evans's restoration. The plan catered to tourist groups as well as to single visitors, and it offered several alternative routes, of varying duration, around the site. It also aimed to provide more information for the visitor on the site. An announcement of the plan, estimated to cost 120 million drachmas, was published in the Greek press on 24 November 1994 (see, for example, *Kathimerini* 1994). According to the press reports, the minister of culture and the general secretary of the Ministry of Culture had approved the spending of 100 million drachmas on the project. As recently as 31 May 1996, however, there was little progress, and a number of archaeologists and other workers responsible for the site issued a statement urging the commencement of maintenance work on the monument (see *AegeaNet* 1996).

23. In the discussion following Evans's paper, the president of the society noted that "caution was necessary, as repairs might be taken in the future for original work" (Evans 1927:267).

24. The position of the Dolphin Fresco, for example, restored above the door of the Queen's Megaron, has been questioned by Robert Koehl, who has argued that it was more likely a floor fresco from the story above (Koehl 1986). Elsewhere, the various phases of the reconstruction of the Stepped Portico, south of the Throne Room, that led up from the Central Court to the upper floor, or Piano Nobile, were carefully recorded in a series of photographs dating from 1904 through 1930 (Brown 1983:pls. 25–27; see also Figs. 7–12 herein). In addition to the steps leading to the upper floor, a further flight gave access either to a second floor or to the roof. With regard to this flight, Brown states, "Mackenzie thought, probably wrongly, that two slabs forming a 'seat' in the Room of the Chariot Tablets were steps from here" (Brown 1983:42).

25. The use of reinforced concrete (*béton armé*) is praised and discussed in detail in Evans (1927); compare Fyfe (1926:479).

References

AegeaNet
1996   Summary report, cited 1 June at AegeaNet
        (http://www.duke.edu/web/jyounger/aegeanet.html).

Aposkitou, M.
1979   Μίνως Καλοκαιρινός · ἔκατο χρόνια ἀπὸ τήν πρώτη ἀνασκαφὴ τῆς Κνωσσοῦ
        (Minos Kalokairinos: Hekato chronia apo ten prote anaskaphe tes Knossou;
        Minos Kalakairinos: One hundred years since the first excavation of Knossos).
        Kretologia 8:81–94.

Bammer, A.
1990   Wien und Kreta: Jugendstil und minoische Kunst. *Jahrbuch des Österreichen
        Archäologischen Instituts* 60:29–151.

Bažant, J.

1992   Minos I. In *Lexicon Iconographicum Mythologiae Classicae,* vol. 6, 570–74.
        Zurich: Artemis.

Bintliff, J. L.

1984   Structuralism and myth in Minoan studies. *Antiquity* 58:33–38.

Brachert, T.

1991   Der Verfall minoisch-mykenischer Naturgips-Inkrustationen. *Restauro: Zeitschrift für
        Kunsttechniken und Museumsgragen* 3:179–82.

Brock, J. K.

1957   *Fortetsa: Early Greek Tombs near Knossos.* Cambridge: Cambridge University Press.

Brown, A.

1983   *Arthur Evans and the Palace of Minos.* Oxford: Ashmolean Museum.

1986   I propose to begin at Gnossos. *Annual of the British School at Athens* 81:37–44.

Cadogan, G.

1976   *The Palaces of Minoan Crete.* London: Methuen.

Castleden, R.

1990   *The Knossos Labyrinth: A New View of the "Palace of Minos" at Knossos.* London:
        Routledge.

Coldstream, J. N., ed.

1973   *Knossos: The Sanctuary of Demeter.* London: British School of Archaeology at Athens.

1991   Knossos: An urban nucleus in the Dark Age? In *La transizione dal Miceneo all'Alto
        Arcaismo: Dal palazzo alla città. Atti del Convegno Internazionale a Roma, 14–19 marzo 1988,*
        ed. D. Musti et al., 287–99. Rome: n.p.

Driessen, J.

1990   *An Early Destruction in the Mycenaean Palace at Knossos: A New Interpretation of the
        Excavation Field-Notes of the South-East Area of the West Wing.* Acta Archaeologica
        Lovanensia Monographiae, vol. 2. Louvain: Katholieke Universiteit Leuven.

Evans, A. J.

1894   Primitive pictographs and a prae-Phoenician script, from Crete and the Peloponnese.
        Journal of Hellenic Studies 14:270–372.

1899–1900 Knossos: Summary report of the excavations in 1900. 1. The Palace. *Annual of the
        British School at Athens* 6:3–70.

1900–1901 The palace of Knossos: Provisional report of the excavations for the year 1901. *Annual
        of the British School at Athens* 7:1–120.

1901–2 The palace of Knossos: Provisional report of the excavations for the year 1902. *Annual
        of the British School at Athens* 8:1–124.

1902–3 The palace of Knossos: Provisional report for the year 1903. *Annual of the British School
        at Athens* 9:1–153.

1903–4 The palace of Knossos. *Annual of the British School at Athens* 10:1–62.

1904–5 The palace of Knossos and its dependencies. Provisional report for the year 1905.
        Annual of the British School at Athens 11:1–26.

1908   The diffusion of pictography and its bearing on the origin of script. In *Anthropology and the Classics: Six Lectures Delivered before the University of Oxford,* ed. R. R. Marett, 9–43. Oxford: Oxford University Press.

1909   *Scripta Minoa: The Written Documents of Minoan Crete with Special Reference to the Archives of Knossos.* Vol. 1, *The Hieroglyphic and Primitive Classes with an Account of the Discovery of the Pre-Phoenician Scripts, Their Place in Minoan Story, and Their Mediterranean Relations.* Oxford: Oxford University Press.

1911–14   The "Tomb of the Double Axes" and associated group, and the Pillar Room and ritual vessels of the "Little Palace" at Knossos. *Archaeologia* 65:59–94.

1921   *The Palace of Minos. A Comparative Account of the Successive Stages of the Early Cretan Civilization as Illustrated by the Discoveries at Knossos.* Vol. 1, *The Neolithic and Early and Middle Minoan Ages.* London: Macmillan.

1927   Work of reconstitution in the palace of Knossos. *Antiquaries Journal* 7:258–67.

1928   *The Palace of Minos. A Comparative Account of the Successive Stages of the Early Cretan Civilization as Illustrated by the Discoveries at Knossos.* Vol. 2, pts. 1, 2. London: Macmillan.

1930   *The Palace of Minos. A Comparative Account of the Successive Stages of the Early Cretan Civilization as Illustrated by the Discoveries at Knossos.* Vol. 3, *The Great Transitional Age in the Northern and Eastern Sections of the Palace: The Most Brilliant Records of Minoan Art and the Evidence of an Advanced Religion.* London: Macmillan.

1935   *The Palace of Minos. A Comparative Account of the Successive Stages of the Early Cretan Civilization as Illustrated by the Discoveries at Knossos.* Vol. 4, pts. 1, 2. London: Macmillan.

Evans, J. D.
1964   Excavations in the Neolithic settlement at Knossos, 1957–1960, Part 1. *Annual of the British School at Athens* 59:132–249.

1971   Neolithic Knossos: The growth of a settlement. *Proceedings of the Prehistoric Society* 37(2):95–117.

1994   The early millennia: Continuity and change in a farming settlement. In *Knossos: A Labyrinth of History. Papers Presented in Honour of Sinclair Hood,* ed. D. Evely, H. Hughes-Brock, and N. Momigliano, 1–20. Athens: British School at Athens.

Evans, Joan
1943   *Time and Chance: The Story of Arthur Evans and His Forebears.* London: Longman's, Green.

Evely, D., H. Hughes-Brock, and N. Momigliano, eds.
1994   *Knossos: A Labyrinth of History. Papers Presented in Honour of Sinclair Hood.* Athens: British School at Athens.

Fabricius, E.
1886   Alterthümer auf Kreta. 4. Funde der mykenäischen Epoche in Knossos. *Mitteilungen des deutschen archäologischen Instituts in Athen* 11:135–49.

Farnoux, A.
1993   *Cnossos: L'archéologie d'un rêve.* Paris: Gallimard.

Furness, A.
1953   The Neolithic pottery of Knossos. *Annual of the British School at Athens* 48:94–134.

Fyfe, T.

1926   The palace of Knossos: An example in conservation. *Journal of the Royal Institute of British Architects,* 26 June:479–80.

Graham, J. W.

1962   *The Palaces of Crete.* (Rev. eds., 1969, 1987.) Princeton, N.J.: Princeton University Press.

Hägg, R., and N. Marinatos, eds.

1987   *The Function of Minoan Palaces. Proceedings of the Fourth International Symposium at the Swedish Institute at Athens, 10–16 June 1984.* Stockholm: Svenska institutet i Athen.

Hallager, E.

1977   *The Mycenaean Palace at Knossos: Evidence for Final Destruction in the IIIB Period.* Stockholm: Medelhavsmuseet.

Harden, D. B.

1983   *Sir Arthur Evans: A Memoir.* Oxford: Ashmolean Museum.

Haussoullier, B.

1880   Vases peints archaïques découverts à Knossos (Crète). *Bulletin de correspondance hellénique* 4:124–27.

Hogarth, D. G.

1899–1900 Knossos: Summary report of the excavations in 1900. 2. Early town and cemeteries. *Annual of the British School at Athens* 6:70–85.

Hood, S.

1987   An early British interest at Knossos. *Annual of the British School at Athens* 82:85–94.

Hood, S., and D. Smyth

1981   *Archaeological Survey of the Knossos Area.* Oxford: British School at Athens.

Hood, S., and W. Taylor

1981   *The Bronze Age Palace at Knossos: Plans and Sections.* London: Thames and Hudson.

Horwitz, S. L.

1981   *The Find of a Lifetime: Sir Arthur Evans and the Discovery of Knossos.* New York: Viking.

Karo, G.

1959   *Greifen am Thron. Erinnerungen an Knossos.* Baden-Baden: B. Grimm.

Kathimerini

1994   *Kathimerini* (Athens), 24 November.

Koehl, Robert B.

1986   A marinescape floor from the palace at Knossos. *American Journal of Archaeology* 90:407–17.

Makropoulos, K. C., J. K. Drakopoulos, and G. A. Tselentis

1988   Seismic hazard assessment and its contribution to the ancient monument protection—a case history in Greece. In *The Engineering Geology of Ancient Works, Monuments, and Historical Sites: Preservation and Protection, Proceedings of an International Symposium Organized by the Greek National Group of the IAEG [International Association of Engineering Geology], Athens, 19–23 September 1988,* ed. P. G. Marinos and G. C. Koukis, vol. 3, 1265–71. Rotterdam: A. A. Balkema Publishers.

Momigliano, N.

1995   Duncan Mackenzie: A Cautious Canny Highlander. In *Klados: Essays in Honour of J. N. Coldstream,* ed. C. Morris, 163–70. London: Institute of Classical Studies.

Moraiti, E., and B. Christaras

1992   Weathering of marly and biogenic limestones used in the antiquities of Crete, Greece: Stratigraphy and mechanical consideration. In *La conservation des monuments dans le bassin méditerranée. Actes du 2ème symposium international, Genève, 19–21 novembre 1991,* ed. D. Decrouez, J. Chamay, and F. Zezza, 483–92. Geneva: Musée d'art et d'histoire.

Morris, S. P.

1992   *Daidalos and the Origins of Greek Art.* Princeton, N.J.: Princeton University Press.

Mosso, Angelo

1907   *The Palaces of Crete and Their Builders.* New York: G. P. Putnam's Sons.

Myres, J.

1951   The palace at Knossos: British estate offered to the Greek government. *Times* (London), 14 July.

Myers, J. W., E. E. Myers, and G. Cadogan

1992   *The Aerial Atlas of Ancient Crete.* Berkeley: University of California Press.

Niemeier, W.-D.

1985   *Die Palaststilkeramik von Knossos: Stil, Chronologie und historischer Kontext.* Archäologischen Forschungen, vol. 13. Berlin: Mann.

Palmer, L. R.

1969   *The Penultimate Palace of Knossos.* Incunabula Graeca, vol. 33. Rome: Edizioni dell'Ateneo.

Palmer, L. R., and J. Boardman

1963   *On the Knossos Tablets.* Oxford: Oxford University Press.

Papageorgakis, J., and E. Mposkos

1988   Building stones of the Minoan palace of Knossos. In *The Engineering Geology of Ancient Works, Monuments, and Historical Sites: Preservation and Protection,* ed. P. G. Marinos and G. C. Koukis, vol. 2, 649–59. Rotterdam: A. A. Balkema Publishers.

Picard, C.

1932   Au pays du griffon: Cnossos ressuscitée. *La revue de l'art* 41:3–18, 49–60, 105–16.

Popham, M. R.

1964   *The Last Days of the Palace at Knossos: Complete Vases of the Late Minoan IIIB Period.* Lund, Sweden: Carl Bloms Boktryckeri.

1970   *The Destruction of the Palace at Knossos: Pottery of the Late Minoan IIIA Period.* Göteborg, Sweden: P. Åström.

Popham, M. R., et al.

1984   *The Minoan Unexplored Mansion at Knossos.* London: Thames and Hudson.

Powell, D.

1973   *The Villa Ariadne.* London: n.p.

Raison, J.

1969   Le grand palais de Knossos: Répertoire photographique et bibliographie. Incunabula Graeca, vol. 34. Rome: Edizioni dell'Ateneo.

1988   *Le palais du second millénaire à Knossos.* Vol. 1, *Le quartier nord.* Études crétoises, vol. 28. Paris: P. Geuthner.

Sackett, L. H., et al.

1992   *Knossos: From Greek City to Roman Colony.* Oxford: British School at Athens.

Shaw, J. W.

1971   Minoan architecture: Materials and techniques. *Annuario della Scuola Archeologica di Atene* 49 (n.s. 33).

Sphere

1926   *The Sphere,* 31 July.

Stanley-Price, N., and S. Sullivan

1995   Conservation of archaeological sites in the Mediterranean region: A conference organized by the J. Paul Getty Trust. *Conservation and Management of Archaeological Sites* 1:127–31.

Stillman, W. J.

1880–81   Extracts from letters of W. J. Stillman, respecting ancient sites in Crete. In *Archaeological Institute of America: Appendix to the Second Annual Report of the Executive Committee,* 41–49.

Warren, P. M., M. R. Jarman, H. N. Jarman, N. J. Shackleton, and J. D. Evans

1968   Knossos Neolithic, Part 2. *Annual of the British School at Athens* 63:239–76.

Ephesus

Martha Demas

D URING THE ROMAN IMPERIAL PERIOD, Ephesus had attained sufficient ascendancy over her sister cities in the region that her citizens could proclaim her "the first and greatest city of Asia Minor." Ephesus achieved this status by virtue of being the capital of the Roman province of Asia, the largest emporium of the region, and a showcase of magnificent public buildings and temples, including the famed Temple of Artemis. Nearly two millennia later, Ephesus can once again claim primacy—now, however, as the "first and greatest" tourist attraction in the region. The twentieth-century pursuits of archaeology and tourism have revitalized the fortunes of this ancient city in a way that could not have been anticipated even a few decades ago. How long Ephesus will sustain its new preeminence as a tourist mecca and still retain its integrity as an archaeological site of great historical significance will depend on decisions made in the present about how best to manage this rich inheritance from the past.

Location and Context

The ruins of Ephesus lie at the heart of the Aegean coast of Turkey, whose shoreline is visible from the island of Samos. Once linked to the sea by its large inland harbor, Ephesus is now seven kilometers from the coast and fifteen kilometers from the modern harbor town of Kuşadası. The largest modern city of the region, İzmir, is seventy-five kilometers to the north. The modern-day visitor to Ephesus arrives by sea to Kuşadası (often via Samos) or overland from İzmir.

The designation *Ephesus* is generally understood to refer to the main urban core of the Roman city, whose remains are visible today nestled between Panayirdağ (Mount Pion) and Bülbüldağ (Mount Coressus). This area, which was the center of activity in the region for centuries during the Hellenistic and Roman periods, has now become the focus of visitors and archaeologists. However, to define Ephesus in such limited geographical terms is to ignore a long and rich history encompassing two millennia of almost continuous inhabitation. The term Ephesus, as used in this article, refers to the larger cultural-historical area that includes not only the Roman city but the Artemisium (comprising the

Temple of Artemis and its immediate surrounds), Saint John's Basilica, the Isa Bey Mosque, and other monuments in and around the modern town of Selçuk, as well as the House of Mary in the mountain forest south of the ancient city (Fig. 1).

Significance of Ephesus

The complexity and challenge of protecting and managing Ephesus lie in its scale, the monumentality and diversity of its architecture, the variety of approaches employed in restoration and interpretation of its monuments in the course of its history of modern interventions, and the number of tourists who now visit the site. Overriding all these challenges, however, is the need to reconcile the multiplicity of often conflicting values attributed to Ephesus today by those who have an interest in the site or who benefit from it in one way or another.

Archaeological and historical values

The archaeological and historical values of Ephesus to generations of scholars and archaeologists are well known and documented. The Artemisium, the Roman city, and the religious monuments have been the greatest focus for scholarly and archaeological activity over the last century and more of investigation.[1] They offer both scholars and visitors the opportunity to witness the physical evolution of a place over two millennia and to contemplate the vicissitudes of that history. Of particular interest in this respect are the many shifts in the location of the city and its eventual demise in response to the progressive silting up of the harbor—the economic lifeline of Ephesus.

 The historical significance of Ephesus lies in its importance as one of the twelve cities of Asia Minor founded by the Ionians in the tenth century B.C.E. and home of one of the most important and long-lived sanctuaries of the ancient world, the Artemisium. Established at least as early as the eighth century B.C.E. and maintaining an ascendancy in the ancient world through the initial incursions of Christianity, the Artemisium was regarded as one of the Seven Wonders of the World.

 During the Roman imperial period, Ephesus was the capital of the province of Asia and was one of the largest and wealthiest of the Asia Minor cities. With its large inland harbor, it became the great mercantile center of the region. The well-preserved remains of this vast city have provided scholars with a wealth of information about private, religious, and civic life in the Hellenistic and Roman periods and late antiquity. Despite the loss of its magnificent harbor through silting, Ephesus today retains to a high degree its integrity as an ancient landscape and as an exemplar of Hellenistic and Roman architecture and urban planning (Fig. 2).

 Archaeological investigations of the religious monuments, in conjunction with historic texts and inscriptions reflecting the rise of Christianity, have also contributed significantly to our understanding of the early history of Christianity and religious architecture in the region.

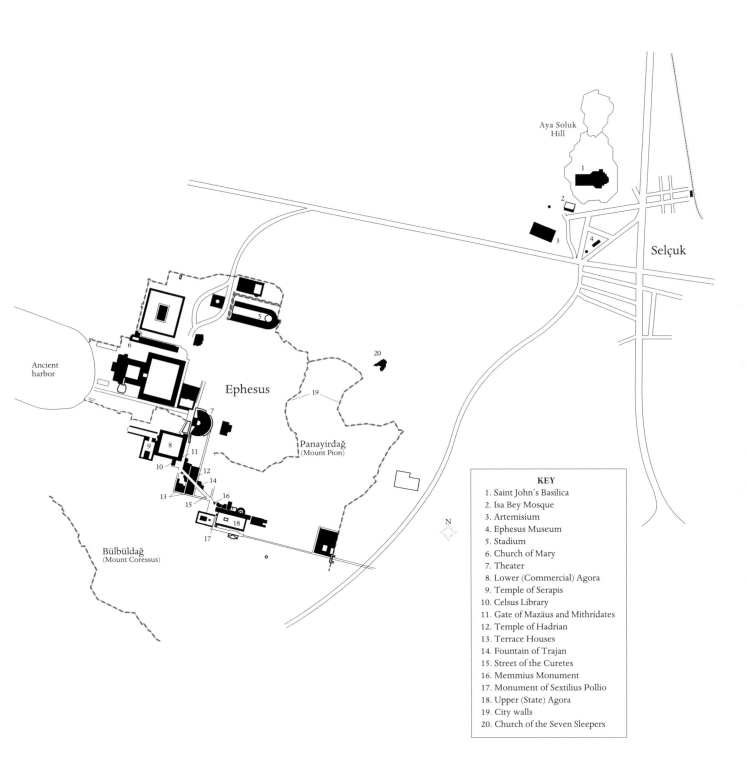

Figure 1
Plan of Ephesus-Selçuk.

Aya Soluk
Hill

Selçuk

Ancient
harbor

Ephesus

Panayirdağ
(Mount Pion)

Bülbüldağ
(Mount Coressus)

N

KEY
1. Saint John's Basilica
2. Isa Bey Mosque
3. Artemisium
4. Ephesus Museum
5. Stadium
6. Church of Mary
7. Theater
8. Lower (Commercial) Agora
9. Temple of Serapis
10. Celsus Library
11. Gate of Mazäus and Mithridates
12. Temple of Hadrian
13. Terrace Houses
14. Fountain of Trajan
15. Street of the Curetes
16. Memmius Monument
17. Monument of Sextilius Pollio
18. Upper (State) Agora
19. City walls
20. Church of the Seven Sleepers

Figure 2
General view of Ephesus. Ephesus retains much of its integrity as an ancient landscape and a model of Hellenistic and Roman architecture and urban planning. From the Hellenistic city walls on Bülbüldağ (Mount Coressus), the plan of the city—with its streets, agora, theater, public buildings, and private houses—is readily apprehended (see color plate 3a).

Social value

In the hierarchy of cultural values attributed to Ephesus, social value ranks very high. The modern town of Selçuk derives its identity and sense of purpose to a large extent from its physical proximity to Ephesus and its role as caretaker of the ruins and host to the multitude of tourists who visit the site every year. The cultural heritage of Ephesus is a source of pride to local inhabitants.

It is, however, the role of Ephesus as the venue for social and cultural events that is critical to understanding the social value of the place for the local population as well as for transient visitors. Three of the ancient monuments have long served a modern social purpose. The great theater of Ephesus has been the venue for two major festivals—the Selçuk-Efes Festival, which features traditional Turkish dancers and musicians, and the International İzmir Festival, which attracts classical musicians and international superstars who regularly fill the theater to its capacity of twenty thousand (Fig. 3). For the past thirty-three years, a traditional local festival—known as the Camel Wrestling Festival—has been held every January in the ancient stadium, making it the longest-running and most-popular Ephesian event of recent times (Fig. 4). Since its restoration in 1978, the Library of Celsus has been used for a variety of more intimate social gatherings and cultural events. These festivals and other events have enhanced the social and cultural life of the local population and have made the site once again part of the civic fabric of a community.

More subtle in its implications is the limited, but direct, contact between Greece and Turkey at the level of everyday interaction among ordinary people. Tourist boats shuttle visitors to Ephesus, taking them from the island of Samos to the harbor town of Kuşadası, in a modern reenactment of the ancient links between these two places. Ephesus is also a persistent reminder of the ancient culture that once dominated the region and continues to inform its interpretation in the present. Contemporary ties, through the ancient city, allow for an awareness—as well as a degree of familiarity and acceptance—between two modern cultures that are severed by political events.

Figure 3

Spectators filling the theater at Ephesus during a performance. For many years the theater was the venue for the International İzmir Festival, which attracted international superstars who regularly filled it to its capacity of twenty thousand. Thus the monument was once again incorporated into the social and civic fabric of a community.

Figure 4

Stadium at Ephesus. The ancient stadium has long been the venue for a popular local event, the Camel Wrestling Festival, which has enhanced the value of Ephesus for the local population.

Symbolic value

As the principal representative of the Hellenistic and Roman cities that once thrived on the coast of Asia Minor, Ephesus is recognized as a symbolic link between Turkey and Europe. For instance, the Library of Celsus—as an embodiment of European values—is used in the marketing campaign for tourism in Turkey, accompanied by the slogan "Discover the Undiscovered Europe." At a time when Turkey has been striving to obtain entry to the European Community, the importance of such national symbols is manifest. At the local level, however, it is the over-life-size statue of the Ephesian Artemis, with her strong links to the Anatolian goddess Cybele, who holds pride of place in the modern town of Selçuk.

On a more mundane but pervasive level is the use of the name Ephesus for product identification and commercial establishments; the term "Efes" (for cigarettes, beer, shops, and so on) provides name recognition and signifies quality.

Figure 5
Monuments symbolizing the religious history of the eastern Mediterranean. From a single vantage point, a visitor can overlook three monuments: the pagan Temple of Artemis (foreground), the Christian Basilica of Saint John (left), and the Muslim Mosque of Isa Bey (right). During much of the year, the re-erected column from the Artemisium is the only sign of this monument's existence, since the rest of the remains are covered by water. The column also serves as a nesting place for storks.

Religious value

The history of Ephesus encapsulates to an extraordinary degree the history of religion in the eastern Mediterranean: pagan, Christian, Muslim. From a single vantage point one can overlook the three monuments that symbolize this history: the Artemisium, Saint John's Basilica, and the Mosque of Isa Bey (Fig. 5). While the pagan worship of Artemis has no more than historical value in the present, the early Christian monuments and events at Ephesus still animate the use of the place today and endow it with contemporary religious value. This is especially true of the two monuments associated with the Virgin Mary.

The Church of Mary (also referred to as the Double Church or Council Church) is the place historically associated with the Council of Ephesus held in 431 C.E., at which Mary's role as Mother of God was debated and affirmed; every October since 1986, a commemorative mass has been held in the partially restored ruins of the church (Figs. 6, 7). The so-called House of Mary (Meryem Ana Evi), a few kilometers south of the ancient city center, has even greater emotive appeal as the place where, according to certain ecclesiastical traditions, Mary spent her final days. As an important center of Marian worship, the House of Mary receives hundreds of thousands of religious pilgrims—Christian and Muslim—every year, thereby carrying on a venerable tradition established by Mary's pagan predecessor, Artemis (Fig. 8).

Many other monuments at Ephesus have sustained religious associations, despite a lack of historical validation. These include the Grotto of Saint Paul on the slope of Bülbüldağ, Saint Paul's Prison, the Tomb of Saint Luke, and the Church of the Seven Sleepers on Panayirdağ.

Aesthetic and natural values

Not only does Ephesus retain much of the integrity of its ancient topography, it also preserves much of the romantic, pastoral quality of ruins in

Figure 6
Church of Mary, Ephesus. Although only partially restored, the church remains a ruin among ruins, with its historical value left intact.

Figure 8, above
House of Mary, outside Ephesus. While the monument—fully reconstructed as a chapel in the 1950s—has extraordinary religious value as a center for the veneration of the Virgin Mary, it has little historical value. The regular use of the place for masses is consistent with its religious significance.

Figure 7, above
Commemorative mass in the Church of Mary. In recognition of the church's religious value, a mass is held annually in the partially restored ruins.

nature—the aesthetic value that attracts so many visitors to archaeological sites. By virtue of their status as protected areas, archaeological sites often become de facto, unplanned ecological preserves, protecting the natural value of a place—sometimes to the detriment of the cultural values—by serving as a refuge for flora and fauna. The Artemisium, whose low-lying ruins are flooded each winter, provides a seasonal habitat for waterfowl and other aquatic wildlife. The single re-erected column of the temple provides a new residential outpost for the storks of the area (Fig. 5), who had long used the Byzantine aqueduct in Selçuk for nesting, as remarked upon by John Turtle Wood in 1870: "The first stork appeared on one of the piers of the aqueduct at Ayasalouk. It was soon followed by others, till every pier was occupied by a pair. Sometimes a quarrel took place, and there was a fight for the possession of a pier, for the sake perhaps of the old nest, which they leisurely built up again with sticks and twigs brought from the surrounding fields" (Wood 1877:160).

Economic value

The parallel development of Ephesus-Selçuk-Kuşadası as a tourist attraction and recreational center has brought a measure of prosperity to the region and has given the site its economic value. There has been a steady increase of visitors to Ephesus: from 276,000 in 1960 (when the first statistics were compiled) to a peak of nearly 1.7 million in 1988 (Fig. 9).

Ephesus is today the most-developed site in the region. The Municipality of Selçuk, the tourism industry, local businesses, and the national treasury all benefit directly or indirectly from the attraction of Ephesus to tourists, scholars, and archaeologists. However, as in many other places, the local and national authorities who are responsible for the protection and maintenance of the site derive little direct economic return from this bounty.

History of Interventions

During the century-long transformation from abandoned ruin to tourist mecca, Ephesus has borne silent witness to the vicissitudes of twentieth-century archaeological and restoration theory and practice and to the growth of the tourist industry. This transformation constitutes the history of modern Ephesus, whose legacy is as important to the long-term preservation of the site as that of ancient Ephesus.[2]

Period 1: 1863–1895

Ephesus has been a compelling presence for adventurers, pilgrims, scholars, and archaeologists for many centuries. What drew the interest of early travelers and of pilgrims on their way to the Holy Land were the associations of Ephesus with the Artemisium and with early Christianity. The ruins of the city had always been partly visible, and what was not visible—the Temple of Artemis, in particular—was endlessly imagined by early visitors; indeed, "the memory of the past may perhaps have led them to indulge too freely their imagination whilst contemplating the few silent walls which remain" (Fellows 1839:274). Early descriptions of the area reveal it as a sleepy, provincial, malaria-ridden place, long cut off from the rest of the world. Nothing could be further from today's "sun and fun" image of the region than Edward Falkener's description of Ephesus in 1845: "The city of Ephesus is . . . a desert place: the 'candlestick has been removed out of this place,'—the flame, the swords, and the pestilence have done their part; and the land is guarded by Divine vengeance from the intrusion of thoughtless man, by the scorpion and centipede, by marshes infested with myriad of serpents, and by attendant fever, dysentery, and ague" (Falkener 1862:5–6).

Figure 9
Visitor statistics for Ephesus. Visitor levels climbed slowly throughout the 1970s and accelerated rapidly in the 1980s to attain a peak of 1,692,000 in 1988. The vulnerability of tourism to political events is seen in the sharp drops in 1974–75, in response to the Cyprus crisis, and again in 1991, during the Gulf War.

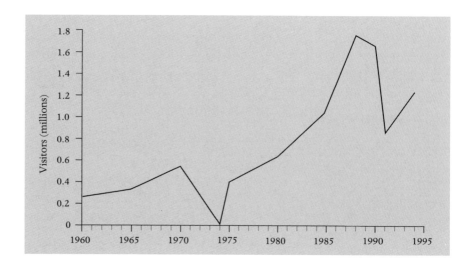

The railway line from Smyrna (İzmir) to Aya Soluk (Selçuk), completed in 1863, opened the region to the outside and made possible the first real archaeological investigation of Ephesus, which was undertaken by J. T. Wood from 1863 to 1874 (Wood 1877). The search for the Artemisium, which drew Wood to Ephesus, constitutes the historical and archaeological focus for this period (Figs. 10, 11). Although Wood found the remains of the temple in 1869, the elucidation of the history of the Artemisium, which spans over a thousand years, has continued almost unabated to the present. These continuous efforts attest not only to the difficulties inherent in excavating this low-lying site, which is covered with water much of the year, but also to the fascination the place holds for scholars and public alike.[3]

Period 2: 1895–1922

The next period in Ephesus's modern history began in 1895, at the beginning of Austrian involvement, which continues to the present under the auspices of the Austrian Archaeological Institute. Although investigation

Figure 10

Searching for the Artemisium. The search for the fabled Temple of Artemis attracted early travelers to Ephesus, but it was not until the arrival of John Turtle Wood in 1863 that the location of the temple beneath centuries of accumulated silt was revealed. Unearthing the historical record of Ephesus was to remain the principal activity at the site for nearly a century.

Figure 11

Reconstruction of the Temple of Artemis. Wood's 1877 reconstruction on paper of the Temple of Artemis is one of many that have been done—both before and after the discovery of the physical remains. One advantage of reconstruction on paper is that it can be easily updated as new information and alternative interpretations emerge.

of the Artemisium continued and was enhanced by D. G. Hogarth's discovery in 1904 of a so-called foundation deposit of gold and ivory, the emphasis began to shift toward the urban center and the Roman public buildings. Much of the lower Roman city (from the Library of Celsus to the Harbor Baths) was investigated at this time. Despite a hiatus in the work during and immediately after the First World War (1914–20), this period witnessed extensive, large-scale clearing to reveal the major monuments and the main outlines of the city. In the course of the clearing, fallen columns were set upright and architectural elements were moved or stored, but no serious attempts were made to restore the monuments.

Interest in the religious monuments of the Ephesus region was given new impetus at this time with the excavation of Saint John's Basilica under G. Sotiriou (1921–22), initiated by the Greek government during its brief occupation of Asia Minor. The fascinating modern history of the House of Mary began in 1891–92, when M. Poulin, superior of the Lazarists of Smyrna, discovered the ruins of a building in the forest south of Ephesus; this structure answered to the description of the House of Mary, as revealed in the early-nineteenth-century vision of a German nun, Anna Katharina Emmerich. To the inhabitants of the nearby village of Şirince—the oft-proclaimed descendants of the Ephesians—the site had long been a place of pilgrimage on 15 August in commemoration of the Assumption of Mary. With the rediscovery of the place by the outside world, annual pilgrimages sanctioned by the archbishop of Smyrna began from İzmir in 1896 and from abroad in 1906.

The end of this period coincides with the end of a long chapter of Greek presence in the region, of which Ephesus itself is a symbol.

Period 3: 1923–1953

In 1923 a new era in modern Turkish history was ushered in with the proclamation of the Turkish Republic. Behind this changed political status was a new national consciousness that had altered in one important respect the way archaeologists pursued their profession. This was the prohibition in 1907 against the transport from Turkey of any excavated finds, a stricture that put an end to the removal of significant architectural and sculptural pieces from the site of Ephesus, which hitherto had been exempted. Among the more significant pieces removed to various museums in Vienna were statues from the Library of Celsus and the Parthian reliefs reused in the fifth-century fountain at the base of the steps of the library (Fig. 12); architectural members from the so-called Rundbau on Panayirdağ and from the Octagon on the Street of the Curetes; and altarpieces from the Artemisium.

Excavation of Roman public buildings continued on a limited scale, but from 1936 to 1953, there was an interruption in work, principally as a result of World War II. Despite the limited activity, this period marks the beginning of a shift toward a more publicly oriented posture. As late as 1936, a traveler to the site could write of Ephesus that it "stands dignified and alone in its death . . . with no sign of life but a goatherd leaning on a broken sarcophagus or a lonely peasant outlined against a mournful

Figure 12
Library of Celsus during excavation, 1903.
The Parthian frieze (seen in the middle
ground) formed part of the fifth-century
reuse of the building; it was removed to
Vienna, where it is currently housed in the
Neue Hofburg.

sunset. Few people ever visit it. Ephesus has a weird, haunted look."[4]
Romantic hyperbole aside, Ephesus at this time was far from being a
destination spot for other than the intrepid traveler. Toward the end of
this period, however, two events occurred to create a public persona for
Ephesus. In 1951 the site of Ephesus was officially opened to visitors—a
sign that tourism had begun to play a role in decisions that would be made
about the site. The proclamation of the dogma of the Assumption of
Mary in 1950 inaugurated a new chapter in the history of the House of
Mary. In 1951, in anticipation of increased visitation, Turkish authorities
constructed a road to the ruined building, and private organizations initiated its reconstruction as a chapel.

Period 4: 1954–1970

This postwar period saw renewed activity in the investigation of Ephesus,
principally of the monuments of the upper city, from the Terrace Houses
to the Magnesian Gate. This period also marks the beginning of restoration and reconstruction at Ephesus. Monuments that underwent partial
or full restoration or reconstruction during this period include the
Church of Mary (1956, 1960s); the Baths of Scholastikia (1956–58); Saint
John's Basilica (1957); the Street of the Curetes (1957); the Temple of
Hadrian (1957–59); the odeon (1960s); the Fountain of Trajan (1962–63);
the Gate of Hercules (1962); the Memmius Monument (1963); the theater
(1965–75); the Monument of Sextilius Pollio (1966); and the Fountain of
Domitian (1970–71).[5]

Figure 13
Temple of Hadrian. The restoration of the
Temple of Hadrian, undertaken in the 1950s,
attempted to reinstate the historic and artistic
integrity of the monument by presenting a
comprehensible and harmonious whole. Not
all elements were incorporated into the
reconstruction, since some (such as the frieze
on the pronaos) were considered too fragile
or too valuable. In some instances, they were
replaced by copies made of white cement.

Figure 14
Monument of Memmius, Ephesus. The 1963
restoration of the Memmius Monument
attempted to convey the fragmentary nature
of monuments and their history of abandonment, collapse, and destruction. Unlike the
treatment of the Temple of Hadrian (Fig. 13),
which invites the viewer to imagine the
monument in its original form, this approach
emphasizes the destruction wrought by the
centuries. The reconstruction deliberately
uses concrete because of the contrast between
its roughly textured finish and the smooth
marble surface of the extant original remains.
Since many of the original members are
missing, the placement of extant pieces only
alludes to the original composition of the
monument.

Three of these projects illustrate the diverse approaches taken to
the problem of presenting an incomplete monument.

The earliest restoration was that of the Temple of Hadrian
(1957–59). This work exemplifies a conceptual approach that was to
become rather standard restoration methodology, one that would later be
promulgated in 1965 in *The Venice Charter* (see Appendix A). The intent of
the restoration was to make the monument comprehensible and to present
a harmonious whole—to reinstate the monument's historic and artistic
integrity. To this end, copies of missing elements and those considered too
precious or fragile to be displayed in their original contexts (such as the
frieze on the pronaos) were incorporated into the temple. White cement
was used for the copies so that they would harmonize with, yet be distinct
from, original materials (Fig. 13).

Only a few years later, the restoration of the Memmius
Monument (1963) reflects a very different approach (Fig. 14). In this
instance, the intent was not to present a harmonious whole but to convey
the fragmented nature of monuments and their history of abandonment,
collapse, and destruction (Bammer 1981, 1988:166ff.). While the Temple of
Hadrian invites the visitor to believe that two thousand years have passed

the monument by without effect, the Memmius Monument tells the story of those intervening years. A deliberately provocative intervention, the reconstruction of the Memmius Monument used concrete, the rough-textured finish of which boldly asserts itself against the smooth marble of the extant original remains. Since many of the original members were missing, the placement of extant pieces only alludes to the original composition of the monument. A similar approach was taken with the restorations of the Monument of Sextilius Pollio (1966) and the Fountain of Domitian (1970–71).

The approach taken with the Fountain of Trajan (1962–63) was an attempt to make a fragmentary monument legible without reconstructing it (Fig. 15a, b). Since most of the vertical elements were missing, the restorers placed the horizontal elements on truncated supports. The result is a presentation of the extant elements of the monument without consideration of its architectural integrity or legibility.

More numerous than these three distinctive projects was the type of "restoration" work whose impetus was primarily to impose some degree of order on the chaos that was revealed upon excavation of a collapsed city of stone (Fig. 16).

It is perhaps no coincidence that during this first period of restoration, tourism became a significant factor, with visitation climbing slowly and steadily, from 276,000 in 1960 to 514,000 in 1969. In response to this increase, the Ephesus Museum in Selçuk was opened in 1964 for the display of objects, sculpture, and architectural elements from the excavations. With the 1967 visit of Pope Paul VI to the House of Mary, the status of this place as a pilgrimage site was enhanced, and visitation increased further.

Figure 15a, b
Fountain of Trajan. This restoration approach attempts to make a fragmentary monument legible without reconstructing it. Since most of the vertical elements were missing, the horizontal elements were placed on truncated supports. This arrangement defies understanding by most visitors, who are neither versed in the nuances of restoration philosophy nor skillful in relating what they see in three dimensions (a) to the two-dimensional reconstruction drawing (b, after H. Pellionis) found in guidebooks and on interpretive signs.

b

a

Figure 16
Excavations in the upper city, 1950s. A major
impetus for much of the "restoration" activity
at a site such as Ephesus derives from the
need to impose some degree of order on the
chaos that is revealed upon the excavation of
a collapsed city of stone.

Figure 16
Excavations in the upper city, 1950s. A major
impetus for much of the "restoration" activity
at a site such as Ephesus derives from the
need to impose some degree of order on the
chaos that is revealed upon the excavation of
a collapsed city of stone.

Period 5: 1971–present

In this period, research interest began to move away from civic life and
public buildings to an exploration of everyday life and private houses, on
the one hand, and to an investigation of the site's early history, on the
other. More restoration projects, some of very large scale, took place
during this period. These included the Library of Celsus (1970–78); the
Terrace of Domitian (1976–77); the Gate of Mazäus and Mithridates
(1978–89); the East Stoa of the Marble Street (1983–84; 1988); the public
latrines (in the Baths of Scholastikia) (1989); and the Gate of Hadrian
(1989–). Other restorations, begun in earlier years, continued: the theater (1988, 1992); the Church of Mary (1985); and Saint John's Basilica
(1974–93). Another project begun during this period was the construction
of a shelter over the Terrace Houses (1979–85).

    The Library of Celsus is the best known of the many restorations
at Ephesus; along with the statue of Artemis, it has become one of the
principal symbols of the site (Fig. 17). Even though it was originally excavated in 1903, the decision to restore the library was not taken until 1970.
The restorers used *The Venice Charter* as their philosophical guide and
referred to their intervention as an anastylosis (see Schmidt, herein, for a
discussion of the Library of Celsus).[6] From the outset the intention was to
restore only the highly ornamented facade, leaving the interior walls as
excavated. The restoration was predicated on the assumption that today's
visitors do not want to see romantic ruins—as exemplified, for instance, in
the Temple of Serapis—but prefer to see the monument as it looked in
ancient times. The restoration was further rationalized on the basis of its
research value for scholars. In 1978 the project was extended to include the
adjacent Gate of Mazäus and Mithridates, with the intention of creating
an architectural ensemble around the central court of the Celsus Library.

    The other major intervention project during this period was the
construction of a permanent shelter to protect the Terrace Houses

Figure 17
Library of Celsus, 1993. The restoration of
the monument in the 1970s was undertaken
on the assumption that today's visitors would
prefer to see it as it looked in ancient times
rather than as a romantic ruin. Since the completion of the restoration, the library has
become one of the principal symbols of
Ephesus and the primary attraction for visitors.

Figure 18
Terrace Houses at Ephesus, with temporary
sheltering. Shortly after excavation, the
houses were covered with temporary roofing
designed to protect the remains from the
weather without obscuring the complex.

(Wiplinger 1990; Schmidt 1988). These terraced, urban apartments contain
wall paintings and mosaic floors left in situ, which, together with the
many objects recovered, provide a vivid picture of the everyday life of
wealthy Ephesians. The houses were excavated over a twenty-five-year
period (1960–85) and protected with temporary roofing until the construction of a permanent shelter began in 1979 (Fig. 18).

Figure 19
Terrace Houses after final sheltering. In 1979
the construction of a permanent shelter,
intended to cover all of the excavated houses,
was started. Because of controversies that
arose about its scale and visual intrusiveness,
the new shelter was completed over only two
of the upper terrace apartments. The permanent shelter over the two terrace houses,
flanked by a pair of modern, high-powered
cranes, typifies the trend toward massive and
costly interventions at archaeological sites
that are primarily aimed at interpreting
monuments to visitors.

The shelter attempts to reconstruct the space of the original
rooms through use of intersecting gabled roofs that make reference to the
ground plan. Reinforced concrete pillars support concrete girders and a
ring beam, which defines the perimeter of the complex and supports a
wooden roofing truss with red tiles (Fig. 19). New wall construction was
carried out in brick (Schmidt 1988:90ff.). Even though it was originally
intended to cover all of the excavated houses, the shelter was completed
over only two of the upper terrace apartments because of controversies
about its scale and visual intrusiveness. The houses have only periodically
been opened to the public—primarily because the mechanism and
resources to keep them open have been lacking.

These two projects exemplify a new phenomenon at Ephesus
and in the world of archaeology—the trend toward massive and costly
interventions in direct response to the demand for interpretation of
monuments to the visiting public. The costs of these projects often far
outstrip the resources available for the traditional archaeological pursuits
of excavation, study, and publication, as well as for the less visible work
of maintenance.

During this period there was also renewed interest in the restoration of religious monuments. Inspired by a vision of the Virgin Mary, the
philanthropist George Quatman sponsored further restoration work with
the Ephesus Museum in Selçuk at the Church of Mary, the House of Mary,
Saint John's Basilica, and the Church of Saint John Prodromos in the
nearby village of Şirince. Another papal visit to the House of Mary, by
John Paul II in 1979, further reinforced its importance as a pilgrimage site.

Visitor levels at Ephesus continued to climb slowly throughout
the 1970s (from 514,000 to 578,000) and accelerated rapidly in the 1980s to
attain a high of 1,692,000 in 1988. Then visitor numbers gradually fell off,
to 1,372,000 in 1994. The vulnerability of tourism to political events is dramatically illustrated in the visitor statistics from Ephesus. Sharp drops in
visitation occurred in 1974–75, at the time of the Cyprus crisis, and again
in 1991 during the Gulf War; visitation has not yet rebounded to previous
levels, possibly because of national political disturbances in the area in
1992–93 (Fig. 9).

The increase in tourism and the concomitant restoration of individual monuments were the impetus for the extensive use of the monuments—particularly the theater, stadium, and Celsus Library—for musical concerts, local festivals, and other events.

Responding to the high number of visitors, authorities undertook management initiatives—first in 1970, in conjunction with the U.S. National Park Service, which resulted in the Ephesus Master Plan (U.S. National Park Planning Project 1970), and again in 1979, under a cooperative program initiated by the Ministry of Culture. Implementation of these plans—which call for the creation of infrastructure for tourism (new parking areas, shuttle systems, and access routes), a new administrative structure, and a proposed reopening of the late-Roman-period harbor channel to allow access from the sea—has been impeded by lack of resources and the plans' unrealistic goals. Paradoxically, the one project that has been implemented was not envisaged in the plans and was not even acceptable to the authorities responsible for the site—but it was favored by other local interests. This was the construction of an airstrip within a buffer zone near the ancient ruins and adjacent to the harbor channel.

Issues Raised by the Site

The issues that emerge most forcefully from a review of the modern history of Ephesus are those that result from the variety of approaches that have been employed in restoration and interpretation of monuments, from the use of ancient monuments in a modern context, and from the challenges posed by mass tourism.

Approaches to the restoration of monuments

One of the distinctions of Ephesus is that it displays a variety of approaches to the problem of making a ruined monument "whole" or "legible"—that is, to the restoration and interpretation of monuments. Ephesus is a veritable laboratory of restoration philosophies and practices, and its monuments illustrate radically different conceptual approaches. The Temple of Hadrian and the Library of Celsus attempt to restore wholeness and integrity to the monument along the lines advocated in *The Venice Charter* (Figs. 13, 17). It is a harmonious approach, in bold contrast to the deliberately disharmonious statement made by the Memmius Monument (Fig. 14), the Fountain of Domitian, and the Monument of Sextilius Pollio. Nature has achieved her own version of the scarred and maimed monument in the untouched ruins of the Temple of Serapis (Fig. 20). The Fountain of Trajan sacrifices comprehension to authenticity in the attempt to re-erect a monument lacking vital elements without reconstructing those elements (Fig. 15a, b).

This eclectic approach to the restoration and interpretation of monuments at Ephesus is organic and unplanned—the result of individual decisions made without reference to any overriding plan, guidelines, or framework for the site. Together with the various rationales behind a particular intervention (whether it be to further research, to attract visitors, to make a philosophical or political statement, or to respond to a religious

Figure 20
Temple of Serapis. Unreconstructed, the Temple of Serapis is nature's own example of a scarred and maimed monument that displays its history of abandonment and collapse. The remains of the temple exemplify the "romantic" ruin, whose value is principally aesthetic rather than didactic.

vision), these restorations have become part of the modern history of Ephesus—so much so, in fact, that many restored monuments are more interesting as modern interpretations of ancient monuments than they are as illustrations of ancient Roman buildings. While this modern history of the monuments has value in its own right, it raises a number of questions: How are decisions made and communicated to the public? Do the restorations provide a consistent and meaningful experience for visitors? Should a modern intervention be retained, even if subsequent research shows it to be incorrect? and Does the modern history of a site have value equal to the ancient history?

The Artemisium poses different questions. The Temple of Artemis, one of the most important monuments at Ephesus, has been the subject of investigation for over a century. And yet it is largely an "invisible" monument, whose single re-erected column is often the only sign of its existence (Figs. 5, 21). The value of the temple lies in its research potential for scholars and in its symbolic power for visitors as one of antiquity's Seven Wonders of the World. But how can these values best be interpreted to the public when so little remains visible?

Figure 21
Artemisium during the summer months. Despite its historical significance and popular appeal as one of antiquity's fabled Seven Wonders of the World, the Temple of Artemis is largely an invisible monument. During the winter, when it is submerged in water (Fig. 5), its single re-erected column is often the only sign of its existence.

Modern use of ancient monuments

The use of ancient monuments at Ephesus for public events and ceremonies has had considerable social and religious value for the local population and foreign visitors, and it also has potential economic value for
local and national authorities (Figs. 3, 4). Modern use, however, is often
very different from the original use of the monument and may even
endanger it, contribute to its deterioration, or require the addition of new
materials to ensure its current stability or modern function. There may
also be an inherent conflict between the social and economic values
derived from the use of the monuments and their historical value.

How should we define "appropriate use" of an ancient monument? What are the criteria and limits that should be applied? Are they
universal? How do we balance conflicting values in making decisions about
the use of a monument? The monuments at Ephesus have recently been
closed to visitors and use because of concerns about stability, safety, and
potential damage. Such concerns, as well as the undercurrent of controversy that has surrounded the monuments' use from the outset, highlight
the necessity of addressing these issues in a comprehensive manner prior
to making decisions about use.

The use of ancient monuments for religious purposes illustrates
the difficulties of reconciling different values. Religious associations with a
monument frequently have their origins in ambiguous traditions. The
associations that adhere to Saint John's Basilica (the tomb of the saint), the
Church of Mary (venue for the Council of Ephesus in 431 C.E.), and the
House of Mary (the final residence of the Virgin Mary) all have tenuous
links to historical events, but there is little evidence to substantiate these
associations. One might even claim that the more tenuous the connection,
the more tenacious the belief. In these cases, the religious value of the
monuments—as a focus of contemporary religious belief—may conflict
with the historical record and, therefore, with the interpretation and use of
the monument in the present. These factors set the scene for a battle
between historian and religious devotee for the heart and soul of the
monument. And in the face of strongly held religious beliefs, the historical
veracity of the association loses its meaning.

One of the presumptions that prevails among champions of particular values is that one value must win out over the other. In cases of
conflict, however, reconciliation of values lies not in favoring one over the
other but in finding a balance that can accommodate present differences
and future changes in the values attributed to a monument. The Church of
Mary is an example of such a reconciliation of historical and religious values (Figs. 6, 7).

Tourism and management

Tourism is undeniably one of the major driving forces behind the development of archaeological sites such as Ephesus. To a large extent, excavation, restoration, and use of monuments are all being spurred on by the
perceived needs of tourists. Allowing tourism to set the agenda for much

Figure 22
Theater at Ephesus. Restored as a historic
monument, the theater was never sufficiently
stabilized for modern use, although it served
as the venue for two major festivals (see
Fig. 3). In recent years, the instability of the
structure has created concern about the safety
of visitors and the conservation of the monument. The theater is now often closed to visitors, pending a decision on how it should be
conserved and used (see color plate 3e).

of what happens on a site without ensuring the mechanisms to cope with
an influx of visitors has ultimately proved to be self-defeating. The shelter
over the Terrace Houses is a case in point. The principal rationale behind
the construction of the shelter was to interpret these well-preserved
houses to the public. A tour of the houses provides one of the most infor-
mative and interesting experiences at Ephesus. And yet the intimate spaces
of these domestic interiors are not amenable to mass tourism—so they
have remained closed to visitors since 1989.

An imposing restoration project such as the Library of Celsus acts
as a magnet at a site, drawing the visitor inexorably toward its preeminence. The impact of a magnet monument on the use of a site can be
significant. Visitors who are drawn to the Celsus Library find themselves in
a cul de sac now that access to the adjacent agora is closed; thus the flow
of traffic through the site's most-visited area is severely impeded. The existence of such imposing monuments as the Library of Celsus and the
Terrace Houses has the further effect of encouraging excessive visitation
to some parts of the site while leaving others neglected.

In many respects Ephesus has become a prisoner of its own success and a victim of rising expectations. Mass tourism has diminished the
quality of the visitors' experience, contributed to the deterioration of the
monuments, and severely strained available resources for maintenance of
the site. Unable to staff the site adequately and stabilize monuments, the
authorities have been forced in recent years to periodically close off large
areas and important monuments—such as the theater (Fig. 22)—to visitors
and use. The goose that laid the golden egg for so many years is in danger
of becoming barren.

A site like Ephesus encourages us to take the long view. A survey
of the modern history of Ephesus over the last 130 years shows the evolution of clear trends. Starting with the initial investigations in 1863, archaeological excavation was the dominant—often the sole—activity for almost
ninety years. Here was the archaeologist's paradise: never-ending discoveries and few distractions or obstacles to hinder the pursuit. By the early
1950s, however, we see the first signs of another constituency—the curious
visitor—about to intrude on paradise (Fig. 23), and in the late 1950s, a new
activity—restoration—that would transform the landscape of paradise.

The confluence of these forces led to the extensive use of the ancient monuments for social and cultural events. Thus was born a new trend, as "genteel" visitation was transformed into mass tourism, and academic restoration gave way to megaprojects designed in part to feed the tourist machine. In this new world, archaeologists have become only one of many constituencies vying to define the significance of Ephesus.

It is difficult to gauge the next trend; it seems certain, however, that Ephesus cannot survive on its present course for another twenty years without a mechanism to contend with the rapid change and increasing complexity that characterize this new world. Conservation and management strategies afford such a mechanism, and they may well be the emerging trend of the future. However, they will require vision and determination to withstand powerful contending pressures—in order to keep the significance of Ephesus intact and allow it to flourish well into the next millennium.

Figure 23

The ubiquitous visitor. Is he contemplating the vicissitudes of Ephesian history, nursing a headache caused by sunstroke, or striking a pose for posterity? Is he aware that his action—repeated by thousands of others— will damage his seat? The lack of understanding about the expectations of visitors to archaeological sites is a serious impediment to the development of effective policies.

Acknowledgments

The author wishes to gratefully acknowledge Selahattin Erdemgil, Anton Bammer, Ulrike Muss, Stefan Karwiese, Mehmet Erol, and Fr. Joe Buttigieg for their generosity in sharing their time, knowledge of Ephesus, and hospitality during the preparation of this paper and visits to the site. Dr. Ulrike Muss undertook the background research and compilation of references, information on the monuments, and images, which together form the backbone of this article.

Notes

1. An accessible, brief overview of the history of Ephesus, early Christianity, the Artemisium, and recent discoveries can be found in *Monde de la Bible* (1990:2–48).

2. For a history of the discovery of Ephesus and the Austrian excavations at the site, see Miltner (1958a:307–14, 1958b), Alzinger (1962), Oberleitner and Lessing (1978:169–93), and Wiplinger and Wlach (1996). Wohlers-Scharf (1994) presents all the official documents and international agreements relating to the excavations of Ephesus.

3. Bammer (1984) provides a historical perspective on the search for the Artemisium; see also Bammer in *Monde de la Bible* (1990:8–15) for a recent overview.

4. H. V. Morton as quoted in Bean (1966:160).

5. For descriptions and critiques of many of the restoration projects, see Miltner (1958a, 1958b, 1959:1–10), Bammer (1988:166ff.), *Monde de la Bible* (1990:33), and Schmidt (1993).

6. For a technical description, philosophical discussion, and critique of the Library of Celsus project, see Hueber (1985:398ff., 1989:111–19), Hueber and Strocka (1975), Fehr (1981:107–25), and Bammer (1981, 1988:166ff.).

References

Alzinger, Wilhelm
1962   *Die Stadt des siebenten Weltwunders: Die Wiederentdeckung von Ephesos.* Vienna: Wollzeilen-Verlag.

Bammer, Anton
1981   Architektur und Klassizismus. *Hephaistos* 3:95–106.

1984   *Das Heiligtum der Artemis von Ephesos.* Graz, Austria: Akademische Druck- und Verlagsanstalt.

1988   *Ephesos: Stadt an Fluß und Meer.* Graz, Austria: Akademische Druck- und Verlagsanstalt.

Bean, George E.
1966   *Aegean Turkey: An Archaeological Guide.* London: Ernest Benn.

Falkener, Edward
1862   *Ephesus and the Temple of Diana.* London: Day and Son.

Fehr, Burkhard
1981   Archäologen, Techniker, Industrielle: Betrachtungen zur Wiederaufstellung der Bibliothek des Celsus in Ephesos. *Hephaistos* 3:107–25.

Fellows, Charles
1839   *A Journal Written during an Excursion in Asia Minor.* London: John Murray.

Hueber, Friedmund
1985   Antike Baudenkmäler als Aufgabengebiet des Architekten. In *Lebendige Altertumswissenschaft. Festgabe für Hermann Vetters.* Vienna: Adolf Holzhausens Nfg.

1989   Die Anastylose-Forschungsaufgabe, Restaurierungs- und Baumaßnahme. *Österreichische Zeitschrift für Kunst und Denkmalpflege* 43:111–19.

Hueber, Friedmund, and V. M. Strocka
1975   Die Bibliothek des Celsus: Eine Prachtfassade und das Problem ihrer Wiederaufrichtung. *Antike Welt* 4:3ff.

Miltner, Franz
1958a   Ephesos, die Stadt der Artemis und des Johannes: Österreichs Ausgrabungsstätte in Anatolien. *Atlantis* 30:307–14.

1958b   *Ephesos, die Stadt der Artemis und des Johannes.* Vienna: Franz Deuticke Verlag.

1959   Denkmalpflege in Ephesos. *Österreichische Zeitschrift für Kunst und Denkmalpflege* 13:1–10.

Monde de la Bible
1990   Ephèse, la cité d'Artémis. *Le Monde de la Bible. Archéologie et histoire* (May/June):2–48.

Oberleitner, Wolfgang, and Erich Lessing
1978   *Ephesos.* Vienna: Carl Ueberreuter Verlag.

Schmidt, Hartwig
1988   *Schutzbauten: Denkmalpflege an archäologischen Stätten.* Stuttgart: Konrad Theiss Verlag.

1993   *Wiederaufbau: Denkmalpflege an archäologischen Stätten.* Stuttgart: Konrad Theiss Verlag.

U.S. National Park Planning Project
1970   *Master Plan for Protection and Use: Ephesus Historical National Park.* N.p.: U.S. National Park Service.

Wiplinger, Gilbert
1990   Restaurierungsprojekte in Ephesos. In *Echo. Festschrift für J. B. Trentini.* Innsbruck: Universität Innsbruck.

Wiplinger, Gilbert, and G. Wlach
1996   *One Hundred Years of Austrian Research.* Vienna: Böhlam-Verlag.

Wohlers-Scharf, Traude
1994   *Die Geschichte der Grabung Ephesos.* Frankfurt am Main: Peter Lang Verlag.

Wood, John Turtle
1877   *Discoveries at Ephesus, Including the Sites and Remains of the Great Temple of Diana.* London: Longmans, Green.

APPENDIX A

Summary of Charters Dealing with the Archaeological Heritage

Martha Demas

Recommendations of the Madrid Conference (1904)

These brief recommendations, the result of the Sixth International Congress of Architects, constitute an early attempt to set down principles of architectural conservation. The recommendations emphasize the importance of minimal intervention in dealing with ruined structures, and of finding a functional use for historic buildings. The document sets forth the principle of unity of style, which encourages restoration according to a single stylistic expression.

Recommendations of the Athens Conference (1931)

The conclusions of the Athens Conference, organized by the International Museums Office, were drafted at the end of the conference on restoration of historic buildings held in Athens in 1931. This document introduced such important conservation concepts and principles as the idea of a common world heritage; the importance of the settings of monuments; and the principle of reintegration of new materials. The recommendations were ahead of their time in calling for the reburial of archaeological remains when their conservation cannot be guaranteed, but they were shortsighted in their recommendation of the use of reinforced concrete for consolidation of ancient monuments.

Carta del restauro italiana (1931)

The principles set forth in the *Carta del restauro* reflect Italian conservation theory and practice. They were established by the Advisory Council for Antiquities and Fine Arts in 1931 to guide restoration work carried out by private and public agencies in Italy. This document and Italian restoration theory in general were major sources of the ideas later expressed in *The Venice Charter*.

Recommendation on International Principles Applicable to Archaeological Excavations (1956)

This document, adopted by the General Conference of Unesco in 1956, established international principles governing the protection and excavation of archaeological sites. With respect to conservation, the document recommends the provision of funds for site maintenance; the careful supervision of the restoration of archaeological remains; a prohibition against removal of monuments without consent; and a provision in the deed of concession to excavate, for the guarding, maintenance, and conservation of the site and its associated objects. The recommendation is not legally binding but has often served as a model for national legislation governing excavation.

International Charter for the Conservation and Restoration of Monuments and Sites (The Venice Charter) (1964, 1965)

The Venice Charter codifies the internationally accepted standards of conservation practice relating to architecture and sites. The document—first developed at the Second International Congress of Architects and Technicians of Historic Monuments, held in Venice in 1964—was officially adopted by the International Council of Monuments and Sites (ICOMOS) in 1965. It sets forth principles of conservation based on the concept of authenticity and the importance of maintaining the historical and physical context of a site or building. *The Venice Charter* has been the most influential international conservation document for the past quarter century.

Convention Concerning the Protection of the World Cultural and Natural Heritage (World Heritage Convention) (1972)

The World Heritage Convention was adopted in 1972 by the General Conference of Unesco. It promotes an international perspective on cultural heritage by inviting member states to nominate heritage places of outstanding universal value as World Heritage Sites. It is intended to encourage national efforts at protecting cultural and natural heritage and to promote international recognition and cooperation in safeguarding the heritage of the world. Another publication, *Operational Guidelines for the Implementation of the World Heritage Convention,* was issued in 1988. These guidelines outline the criteria that a site must meet to be included on the World Heritage List.

Charter of Cultural Tourism (1976)

The *Charter of Cultural Tourism* is the result of the ICOMOS Tourism Committee seminar on contemporary tourism and humanism, held in 1976. It outlines an approach to cultural tourism that recognizes sites and monuments as sources of economic benefit and cultural education. The approach encourages educating tourists (including children, the tourists of the future) about the value of monuments and training those responsible for developing and implementing tourist use of heritage sites.

Australia ICOMOS Charter for the Conservation of Places of Cultural Significance (The Burra Charter) (1979)

The Burra Charter is a national charter that establishes principles for the management and conservation of cultural sites in Australia. The charter was adopted by Australia ICOMOS in 1979. The charter is particularly important for its definition of cultural significance and for the process set forth for using cultural significance to manage and conserve cultural sites. It provides an example of how international principles can be adapted to the values and needs of a particular nation or of particular cultural groups within that nation.

Charter for the Protection and Management of the Archaeological Heritage (ICAHM Charter) (1990)

This document, the work of the ICOMOS International Committee on Archaeological Heritage Management (ICAHM), is among the most recent of international charters. It was created in response to the increasing threats to archaeological sites worldwide, especially from looting and land development. The charter attempts to establish principles and guidelines of archaeological heritage management that have global validity and can be adapted to national policies and conditions.

Charter for Sustainable Tourism (1995)

This charter emerged from the World Conference on Sustainable Tourism held in 1995. It holds that tourism development must be sustainable—that is, "ecologically bearable in the long term, as well as economically viable, and ethically and socially equitable for local communities." Achievement of this goal will require respect for the fragility of the cultural and natural heritage, recognition of local interests, contribution to the local economy, acceptance of participation from all sectors and levels, and creation of appropriate planning and management mechanisms. The charter also calls for the diversification of opportunities and forms of tourism, a reduction in tourism's environmental impact, and the adoption of codes of conduct by the tourist industry.

APPENDIX B

Conference Participants

The entries below reflect affiliations of participants at the time of the conference.

Selma Al-Radi
Institute of Fine Arts
New York University
New York, New York
U.S.A.

Suad Amiry
Director
RIWAQ Centre for Architectural Conservation
Ramallah
Palestine

Camille Asmar
Directeur Général
Direction Générale des Antiquités
Beirut
Lebanon

Sid Ahmed Baghli
Chef de Cabinet
Ministère de la Culture
Algiers
Algeria

Anton Bammer
Oberrat
Österreichisches Archäologisches Institut
Vienna
Austria

Panagiotis Barmpalias
Head, Programming and Design Office
National Tourism Organization of Greece
Athens
Greece

Aicha Ben Abed
Chercheur
Institut National du Patrimoine
Tunis
Tunisia

Pierre Bikai
Director
American Center of Oriental Research
Amman
Jordan

Ghazi Bisheh
Director General
Department of Antiquities
Ministry of Tourism and Antiquities
Amman
Jordan

Anna Maria Bombaci
Dirigente Tecnico Archeologo
Responsabile Sezione Archeologica
Soprintendenza per i Beni Culturali e Ambientali di
Enna
Enna, Sicily
Italy

Anthony Bonanno
Professor and Head
Department of Archaeology
University of Malta
Msida
Malta

Mounir Bouchenaki
Director, Division of Cultural Heritage
Unesco

Mohammed Boukli-Hacene
Directeur Adjoint, Sites et Monuments Historiques
Ministère de la Culture
Algiers
Algeria

Brigitte Bourgeois
Conservateur du Patrimoine
Service de Restauration des Musées de France
Versailles
France

Neritan Ceka
Director
Qendra e Kërkimere Arkeologjike
Tirana
Albania

Demos Christou
Director
Department of Antiquities
Nicosia
Cyprus

Miguel Angel Corzo
Director
The Getty Conservation Institute
Los Angeles, California
U.S.A.

William D. E. Coulson
Director
American School of Classical Studies
Athens
Greece

Abdelaziz Daoulatli
Directeur Général
Institut National du Patrimoine
Tunis
Tunisia

Matilde De Angelis d'Ossat
Archaeologist
Soprintendenza Archeologica di Roma
Rome
Italy

Martha Demas
Acting Director, Special Projects
The Getty Conservation Institute
Los Angeles, California
U.S.A.

Christos Doumas
Professor of Archaeology
Department of Philosophy
University of Athens
Athens
Greece

Amir Drori
Director of Antiquities
Israel Antiquities Authority
Jerusalem
Israel

Cevat Erder
Professor
Faculty of Architecture
Middle East Technical University
Ankara
Turkey

Román Fernández-Baca Cásares
Director
Instituto Andaluz del Patrimonio Histórico
Consejería de Cultura
Junta de Andalucía
Seville
Spain

Abderrazak Gragueb Chatti
Président Directeur Général
Agence Nationale d'Exploitation et de Mise en Valeur
du Patrimoine Archéologique et Historique
Tunis
Tunisia

Sophocles Hadjisavvas
Curator of Ancient Monuments
Department of Antiquities
Nicosia
Cyprus

Suzy-Marie Hakimian
Chef de la Section des Musées
Direction Générale des Antiquités
Beirut
Lebanon

Donald R. A. Hankey
Architect
Gilmore Hankey Kirke Ltd.
London
United Kingdom

David Harnik
General Director
Israel Government Tourist Corporation
Jerusalem
Israel

Uta Hassler
Archaeologist
Karlsruhe
Germany

Zahi Hawass
Director General of Giza Pyramids and Saqqara
Supreme Council of Antiquities
Cairo
Egypt

Vassos Karageorghis
Director
Archaeological Research Unit
University of Cyprus
Nicosia
Cyprus

Abid Keramane
Président Directeur Général
Opérateur National Algerien du Tourisme
Algiers
Algeria

Hermann Kienast
Assistant Director
Deutsches Archäologisches Institut
Athens
Greece

Amos Kloner
Director of Bet Guvrin Project
Bar-Ilan University
Jerusalem
Israel

Manolis Korres
Director
Parthenon Restoration Project
Ministry of Culture
Athens
Greece

Marc Laenen
Director-General
ICCROM

Vassilis Lambrinoudakis
Professor of Archaeology
Faculty of Philosophy
University of Athens
Athens
Greece

Colin MacDonald
Knossos Fellow
British School of Archaeology at Athens
Knossos, Crete
Greece

Margaret Mac Lean
Director, Documentation Program
The Getty Conservation Institute
Los Angeles, California
U.S.A.

Kamel O. Mahadin
Chairman
Department of Architecture
University of Jordan
Amman
Jordan

Alessandra Melucco-Vaccaro
Soprintendente Archeologo
Ministero per i Beni Culturali e Ambientali
Rome
Italy

Phryne Michael
Director-General
Cyprus Tourism Organisation
Nicosia
Cyprus

Demetrios Michaelides
Associate Professor
Archaeological Research Unit
University of Cyprus
Nicosia
Cyprus

Anthony Pace
Curator
National Museum of Archaeology
Valletta
Malta

Clairy Palyvou
Architect-Archaeologist
Athens
Greece

Guri Pani
Architect
Institute of Cultural Monuments
Tirana
Albania

John Papadopoulos
Associate Curator of Antiquities
The J. Paul Getty Museum
Malibu, California
U.S.A.

Jerry Podany
Conservator of Antiquities
The J. Paul Getty Museum
Malibu, California
U.S.A.

Georgios Rethemiotakis
Assistant Director
Heraklion Museum
Heraklion, Crete
Greece

Hartwig Schmidt
Professor
Technische Hochschule Aachen
Aachen
Germany

Francesco Scoppola
Architect
Soprintendenza Archeologica di Roma
Rome
Italy

Fayez Shoukry
Undersecretary for Planning
Egyptian Tourist Authority
Cairo
Egypt

Valter Shtylla
Director
Institute of Cultural Monuments
Tirana
Albania

Renée Sivan
Cultural Tourism Consultant
Jerusalem
Israel

Giora Solar
Director, Conservation Division
Israel Antiquities Authority
Jerusalem; and
Director Designate, Special Projects
The Getty Conservation Institute
Los Angeles, California
U.S.A.

Edmond Spaho
Vice Minister for Tourism
Ministry of Construction and Tourism
Tirana
Albania

Nicholas Stanley-Price
Deputy Director, Training Program
The Getty Conservation Institute
Los Angeles, California
U.S.A.

Sharon Sullivan
Executive Director
Australian Heritage Commission
Canberra
Australia

Daniel Therond
Principal Administrative Officer
Council of Europe
Strasbourg
France

Marta de la Torre
Director, Training Program
The Getty Conservation Institute
Los Angeles, California
U.S.A.

Marion True
Curator of Antiquities
The J. Paul Getty Museum
Malibu, California
U.S.A.

Timocin Tulgar
Archaeological Consultant
Ministry of Tourism
Ankara
Turkey

John Walsh
Director
The J. Paul Getty Museum
Malibu, California
U.S.A.

Authors

Marta de la Torre has been the director of the Training Program at the Getty Conservation Institute since 1985. From 1981 to 1985 she was coordinator of Special Projects of the International Council of Museums in Paris. She studied art history at George Washington University and management at the American University.

Margaret Mac Lean has been director of the Documentation Program at the Getty Conservation Institute since 1993. Prior to this appointment, she was senior coordinator of the Training Program of the GCI, and earlier, she was executive director of the Center for Field Research at Earthwatch. She studied anthropology, archaeology, and architecture at the University of California, Berkeley.

Sharon Sullivan is the executive director of the Australian Heritage Commission. She was previously with the New South Wales National Parks and Wildlife Service. Having studied history and prehistory, she has taught cultural heritage management in the United States, Australia, and China, and has developed natural heritage conservation policies in Australia.

Christos Doumas has been professor of archaeology at the University of Athens since 1980 and was with the Department of Antiquities for twenty-five years. He studied history and archaeology in Athens and London. He is a member of Academia Europaea, Society of Antiquaries (London), the German Archaeological Institute, ICOMOS, and the Archaeological Society at Athens. He is currently director of the excavations at Akrotiri.

Hartwig Schmidt has been professor of conservation of historic buildings at the Faculty of Architecture of the Technical University in Aachen, Germany, since 1993. From 1979 to 1983 he carried out a research assignment at the German Institute of Archaeology in Berlin, studying the conservation of archaeological sites. In 1984 and 1985, he was head of the research group at the Institute of Conservation in Berlin. From 1985 to 1993, he was head of the Research and Documentation Center at the University of Karlsruhe, working on the special research program Conservation of Historically Important Buildings. He is a member of ICOMOS and of several professional groups in conservation.

Renée Sivan is a heritage presentation specialist, museum planner, and developer of historical sites. She is in charge of presentation and interpretation of major archaeological sites developed by the Israel National Parks Authority and the Israel Government Tourist Corporation. In addition, she lectures on heritage presentation at Haifa University, Haifa, as well as at academic institutions in Europe. For fifteen years, she served as chief curator of the Tower of David Museum of the History of Jerusalem. She obtained her master's degree in archaeology at the Hebrew University of Jerusalem, where she taught archaeology for seventeen years.

Nicholas Stanley-Price is now an independent consultant in cultural heritage preservation. He studied ancient history and prehistory at Oxford University, completing a doctoral dissertation on the early settlement of Cyprus. After ten years of archaeological fieldwork and administration in the Middle East, he was on the staff of the International Centre for the Study of the Restoration and Preservation of Cultural Property (ICCROM) in Rome, from 1982 to 1986. He was deputy director of the Training Program at the Getty Conservation Institute from 1987 to 1995.

John K. Papadopoulos is associate curator of antiquities at the J. Paul Getty Museum. Before his appointment in 1994, he was deputy director of the Australian Archaeological Institute at Athens and assistant professor of archaeology at the University of Sydney. He is also deputy director of the excavations at Torone in northern Greece.

Martha Demas joined the Getty Conservation Institute in 1990 as a fellow in the Training Program. In 1992 she joined Special Projects, where she is currently serving as project manager. She studied Aegean archaeology at the University of Cincinnati and historic preservation at Cornell University.

Illustration Credits

Grateful acknowledgment is extended to the following institutions and individuals for permission to reproduce the illustrations in this volume.

Color Plates

Plates 1a, 1b, 2a–2d, 3b, 3d, 3e: G. Aldana/GCI. Plate 1c: Erich Lessing/Art Resource, N.Y. Plate 1d: Scala/Art Resource, N.Y. Plates 3a, 3c: Photographs by M. Demas.

Part One

Doumas, "Management Considerations at a Mediterranean Site: Akrotiri, Thera"

Figures 1–17: Courtesy of the Archaeological Society in Athens, Excavations at Thera.

Schmidt, "Reconstruction of Ancient Buildings"

Figure 1: Courtesy of the Getty Research Institute for the History of Art and the Humanities, Resource Collections, Los Angeles, Calif. Figures 2a, 2b, 3, 5, 9–12, 14: Photographs by H. Schmidt. Figure 4: Courtesy of the American School of Classical Studies at Athens, Agora Excavation. Figures 6, 7: Courtesy of Deutsches Archäologisches Institut, Athens. Figure 8: Courtesy of Österreichisches Archäologisches Institut, Vienna. Figure 13: Courtesy of Lejre Research Center, Lejre, Denmark. Figure 15: Courtesy of York Archaeological Trust for Excavation and Research Limited, York, England. Figure 16: Courtesy of Plimoth Plantation, Plymouth, Mass.; photographer: Gary Andrashko.

Sivan, "The Presentation of Archaeological Sites"

Figures 1–2, 9–12: Photos courtesy of R. Sivan. Figures 3–8: Photos by Gabi Laron; used with permission.

Figure 1: Beth Shearim, Israel; a project of the Israel National Parks Authority, 1996; interpretation and conceptual design: Renée Sivan; design: Dorit Harel, Harel Designers; models: Adam Braun, Tip Top Studio. Figure 2: Beth Shean, Israel; a project of the Beth Shean Tourist Development Authority, the Israel Government Tourist Corporation, the Israel Antiquities Authority, and the National Parks Authority, 1996; interpretation and conceptual design: Renée Sivan; design: Dorit Harel, Harel Designers; model maker: Pessah Ruder. Figures 3–8: Avdat, Israel; a project of the Israel National Parks Authority, 1993; interpretation and conceptual design: Renée Sivan; set and graphic design: Dorit Harel, Harel Designers; artists: David Gershtein, Yael Calderon; model maker: Pessah Ruder. Figure 9: Tel Dan, Israel; a project of the Israel Government Tourist Corporation and the Israel Antiquities Authority, 1994; interpretation and conceptual design: Renée Sivan; set and graphic design: Ronit Lambrozo. Figure 10: Tel Dan, Israel; a project of the Israel Government Tourist Corporation and the Israel Antiquities Authority; conceptual design and conservation architecture by Giora Solar. Figure 11: Tel Dan, Israel; a project of the Israel Government Tourist Corporation and the Israel Antiquities Authority; interpretation and conceptual design: Renée Sivan; designer: Ronit Lambrozo.

Figure 12: Jerusalem, Old City; a project of the Jewish Quarter Reconstruction and Development Company, 1983; interpretation and presentation consultant: Renée Sivan; design: Dorit Harel, Harel Designers; architect: Yoel Bar-Dor.

Part Two

Stanley-Price, "The Roman Villa at Piazza Armerina, Sicily"

Figure 1: After Carandini, Ricci, and De Vos 1982:fig. 2; courtesy of S. F. Flaccovio Editore, Palermo. Figure 2: Scala/Art Resource, N.Y. Figure 3: Erich Lessing/Art Resource, N.Y. Figures 5, 6: Courtesy of Fototeca Unione, American Academy in Rome. Figure 7: Courtesy of Foto Aeree, Turin, Italy. Figure 8: Duncan Edwards/National Geographic Image Collection. Figures 9, 11, 12: G. Aldana/GCI. Figure 10: N. Stanley-Price/GCI. Figure 13: Courtesy of Unesco, ©1961. Figures 14–16: Photographs by N. Stanley-Price.

Papadopoulos, "Knossos"

Figure 1: After Myers, Myers, and Cadogan 1992:2–3; courtesy of J. W. Myers. Figure 2: After Hood and Smyth 1981, courtesy of the British School at Athens. Figure 3: After A. J. Evans, courtesy of the British School at Athens. Figures 4–26: Courtesy of the Ashmolean Museum, University of Oxford. Figures 27–29: Photographs by J. Papadopoulos.

Demas, "Ephesus"

Figures 2, 6, 20–22: Photographs by M. Demas. Figures 3, 7, 8: Photo Tuncer, Selçuk. Figure 4: Courtesy of Ephesus Museum, Selçuk. Figures 5, 12, 15b, 16, 18: Courtesy of Österreichisches Archäologisches Institut, Vienna. Figures 10, 11: After Wood 1877. Figures 13–15a, 17, 19, 23: G. Aldana/GCI.